Manage Partitions with GParted How-to

A task-based, step-by-step guide that empowers you
to use your disk space effectively

Curtis Gedak

PUBLISHING

BIRMINGHAM - MUMBAI

Manage Partitions with GParted How-to

First published: November 2012

Production Reference: 1161112

Published by Packt Publishing Ltd.
Livery Place
35 Livery Street
Birmingham B3 2PB, UK.

ISBN 978-1-84951-982-3

www.packtpub.com

Credits

Author

Curtis Gedak

Reviewers

Andrew Bradford

Peter Wu

Acquisition Editor

Mary Nadar

Commissioning Editors

Priyanka Shah

Yogesh Dalvi

Technical Editor

Vrinda Amberkar

Project Coordinator

Shraddha Bagadia

Proofreader

Lydia May Morris

Production Coordinator

Prachali Bhiwandkar

Cover Work

Prachali Bhiwandkar

Cover Image

Conidon Miranda

About the Author

Curtis Gedak has managed the GParted project for the past 4 years, coordinating volunteer efforts and resources, managing releases, maintaining the website, developing new features, fixing bugs, and much more. For over 2 decades, Curtis developed a solid set of technical and management skills while working for a variety of companies in industries such as utilities, agriculture, and oil and gas. During this time he specialized in applying relational database technology, managing heterogeneous environments, and developing applications in a multitude of programming languages. With his strong interpersonal skills and sound technical ability he has been instrumental in the success of many projects. Curtis holds a Bachelor of Science degree in Computer Engineering from the University of Alberta.

I would like to thank the Packt Publishing team for their help in creating this book. They provided advice on formatting and layout, constructive criticism, and guidance along the way. I would also like to extend special thanks to Linda Temple, my spouse, who has been very generous with her time, enthusiasm, and support while I wrote this book. Her editing efforts toward style and clarity, along with help from the Packt Publishing team have enabled me to create a better book.

About the Reviewers

Andrew Bradford has been a developer on the Cross Linux From Scratch (`http://cross-lfs.org`) project and an active participant in the BeagleBoard.org community (`http://beagleboard.org`) since 2010. He's been using Linux since RedHat 7 and since then, except for 1 year with a Mac, has been running Linux on the desktop quite successfully. His current interests involve Debian, embedded Linux, flash memories, and Ruby on Rails.

> I'd like to thank my wife, Meghan, and my daughter, Erin. They're both amazing and they inspire me every day.

Peter Wu is a Software Science student at the University of Technology at Eindhoven (The Netherlands). He is an enthusiastic supporter of open source software, helping other users and contributing code. Beyond installing and administrating various systems with Linux distributions, he has also been required to make sane partitioning schemes. For this purpose he uses many tools, including GParted.

www.PacktPub.com

Support files, eBooks, discount offers and more

You might want to visit www.PacktPub.com for support files and downloads related to your book.

Did you know that Packt offers eBook versions of every book published, with PDF and ePub files available? You can upgrade to the eBook version at www.PacktPub.com and as a print book customer, you are entitled to a discount on the eBook copy. Get in touch with us at service@packtpub.com for more details.

At www.PacktPub.com, you can also read a collection of free technical articles, sign up for a range of free newsletters and receive exclusive discounts and offers on Packt books and eBooks.

http://PacktLib.PacktPub.com

Do you need instant solutions to your IT questions? PacktLib is Packt's online digital book library. Here, you can access, read and search across Packt's entire library of books.

Why Subscribe?

- ▶ Fully searchable across every book published by Packt
- ▶ Copy and paste, print and bookmark content
- ▶ On demand and accessible via web browser

Free Access for Packt account holders

If you have an account with Packt at www.PacktPub.com, you can use this to access PacktLib today and view nine entirely free books. Simply use your login credentials for immediate access.

Table of Contents

Preface

Manage Partitions with GParted is a practical, hands-on guide that provides step-by-step instructions, including screenshots, to effectively use your hard drive.

With this book you start with simple tasks that help you to identify drives and partitions. Next you progress to tasks covering the basics of how to grow, shrink, move, and copy partitions without data loss. You finish with advanced tasks that leverage the basic tasks to prepare for new operating systems, migrate space between partitions, and share data among Windows, GNU/Linux, and Mac OS X.

By following through the tasks, from basic to advanced, this book will empower you with the knowledge and tools to manage partitions with GParted.

What this book covers

Creating live media and running GParted (Must know), introduces the best way to access all of the features of GParted and walks you through the steps to create and boot your very own GParted Live CD.

Identifying proper disk device (Must know), describes how to identify a variety of disk device types through the GParted application so that you can be confident in selecting the correct device.

Identifying partitions and actions available (Must know), points out how to distinguish between different partitions and the types of operations available, increasing your knowledge of the potential options open to you for partition editing.

Checking and repairing a partition (Should know), discloses how to spot problems with partitions and outlines how you can approach resolving these problems.

Getting space by shrinking a partition (Should know), expresses how to locate partitions with unused space, leading you through the steps to free up this space for use in other areas.

Creating a new partition (Should know), describes the different types of partitions and shows you how to create a new partition and toggle partition flags.

Moving a partition (Become an expert), points out the implications of moving a partition, outlining how you can move a partition and address potential issues.

Adding space by growing a partition (Should know), details how to increase a partition's size, enabling you to resolve issues when a partition is short of space.

Formatting a partition (Should know), explains why you might wish to format an existing partition and the steps to accomplish this task.

Preparing a new disk device for use (Become an expert), covers which type of partition table to use with different operating systems and firmware, and demonstrates how you can create a new partition table.

Copying a partition (Become an expert), outlines the impact of duplicate UUID and label issues, showing you the steps to copy a partition and address these considerations.

Deleting a partition (Should know), describes the steps to delete a partition and outlines how you can address a potential unexpected outcome.

Moving space between partitions (Become an expert), reveals how you can use a combination of recipes to migrate free disk space to where it is most needed.

Preparing for dual boot with GNU/Linux (Become an expert), breaks out the steps to prepare your disk partitions, including an example of how to install a popular GNU/Linux distribution and therefore enabling you to share files between Windows and Linux.

Adding space to GPT RAID (Become an expert), discloses how to resolve a common problem that occurs when you add storage space to a GPT RAID.

Rescuing data from a lost partition (Become an expert), covers the steps needed to attempt rescuing data from a lost partition, enabling you to try recovering from accidental partition deletion.

Appendix: *Tips and tricks,* outlines additional tasks you can do with GParted, such as maintaining a Mac OS X hybrid partition table, editing iPod partitions, and adding space to virtual machines.

What you need for this book

You will need a basic understanding that disk devices can be divided into separate areas, called partitions, and that these partitions can be used for different purposes.

To follow the recipes in this book you will need an x86 or x86_64 based computer running an operating system, such as Windows, GNU/Linux, or Mac OS X, and a copy of GParted Live (software available for free download from the Internet).

To create your own bootable GParted live CD you will need access to a CD or DVD writer, CD/DVD "burning" software, a blank CD-R/RW disk, and a connection to the Internet.

Alternatively, if your computer does not have a CD/DVD drive, a blank USB flash drive can be used to install a bootable GParted Live image.

Who this book is for

Are you a computer enthusiast keen to maximize your computer's potential?

Have you ever wanted to run multiple operating systems, store data separate from the OS, or otherwise improve the effectiveness of your disk space?

If so, this book is for you.

Conventions

In this book, you will find a number of styles of text that distinguish between different kinds of information. Here are some examples of these styles, and an explanation of their meaning.

Code words in text are shown as follows: "Download the disk image file `gparted-live-w.x.y-z.iso` for the latest stable release of GParted Live from the GParted website."

Any command-line input or output is written as follows:

```
sudo mkdir /mnt/myusb
```

New terms and **important words** are shown in bold. Words that you see on the screen, in menus or dialog boxes for example, appear in the text like this: "To select a device, go to the **GParted | Devices** menu option and select a device of the correct size".

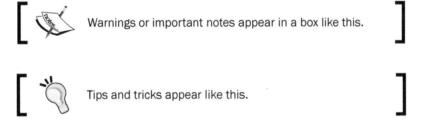

> Warnings or important notes appear in a box like this.

> Tips and tricks appear like this.

Reader feedback

Feedback from our readers is always welcome. Let us know what you think about this book—what you liked or may have disliked. Reader feedback is important for us to develop titles that you really get the most out of.

To send us general feedback, simply send an e-mail to `feedback@packtpub.com`, and mention the book title via the subject of your message.

If there is a topic that you have expertise in and you are interested in either writing or contributing to a book, see our author guide on www.packtpub.com/authors.

Customer support

Now that you are the proud owner of a Packt book, we have a number of things to help you to get the most from your purchase.

Downloading the example code

You can download the example code files for all Packt books you have purchased from your account at http://www.PacktPub.com. If you purchased this book elsewhere, you can visit http://www.PacktPub.com/support and register to have the files e-mailed directly to you.

Errata

Although we have taken every care to ensure the accuracy of our content, mistakes do happen. If you find a mistake in one of our books—maybe a mistake in the text or the code—we would be grateful if you would report this to us. By doing so, you can save other readers from frustration and help us improve subsequent versions of this book. If you find any errata, please report them by visiting http://www.packtpub.com/support, selecting your book, clicking on the **errata submission form** link, and entering the details of your errata. Once your errata are verified, your submission will be accepted and the errata will be uploaded on our website, or added to any list of existing errata, under the Errata section of that title. Any existing errata can be viewed by selecting your title from http://www.packtpub.com/support.

Piracy

Piracy of copyright material on the Internet is an ongoing problem across all media. At Packt, we take the protection of our copyright and licenses very seriously. If you come across any illegal copies of our works, in any form, on the Internet, please provide us with the location address or website name immediately so that we can pursue a remedy.

Please contact us at copyright@packtpub.com with a link to the suspected pirated material.

We appreciate your help in protecting our authors, and our ability to bring you valuable content.

Questions

You can contact us at questions@packtpub.com if you are having a problem with any aspect of the book, and we will do our best to address it.

Manage Partitions with GParted How-to

Welcome to *Manage Partitions with Gparted* where we will lead you on a path to knowledge and discovery that will empower you to take control of your disk storage partitions.

Your first question might be—Why would this be of interest to me?

That is a good question.

- ▶ Have you ever run out of storage space on your C: drive, while having plenty of free space in your D: drive?
- ▶ Perhaps you have an interest in installing a new operating system, or upgrading your current one?
- ▶ Or, maybe you wondered if there is a way to make computer maintenance tasks quicker, or data backup more manageable?

This book will help you meet these challenges by providing the steps and knowledge needed to successfully manage your disk device partitions.

In the beginning...

In the early days of computing and disk storage devices, file system and partition tools were very basic. You could create a partition, format the partition with a file system, and read and write data to the file system. For a long time, these basic tools were all that was available.

As disk storage grew, a need arose to be able to add and change partitions to better utilize the extra storage space. However, resizing a partition and file system was not possible.

Fortunately a number of people who believed in Free Software took it upon themselves to address these shortcomings. Some researched and developed tools to permit editing partitions. Others focused on tools to resize file systems without losing the contents. These tools were then published as Free Software with Open Source licenses, enabling all of us to use and share this software with our friends, family, and co-workers.

Many of these partition and file system tools are available only as text-based commands. To reach a wider audience, the GParted team saw a need for making these tools easier to use. This resulted in the creation of GParted, which provides a graphical interface to these partition libraries and file system tools.

GParted software

In the recipes that follow, we will be using the GParted application from live media containing the GParted Live image.

GParted Live is a small bootable GNU/Linux distribution for x86- and x86_64-based computers that enables you to use all the features of the GParted application on Windows, GNU/Linux, and Intel-based Mac OS X computers.

Importance of computer system backups

Editing partitions has the potential to cause loss of data; there is always the possibility that something could go wrong due to software bugs, hardware failure, or power outage.

As such you are strongly advised to backup your computer system. Backup, test your backups, and backup again. Believe me, there might come a time when you will be glad you did this.

There are many different ways to backup your computer system. Some people make a complete image backup of their storage devices. Others such as myself backup the data only, with the realization that if something goes horribly wrong then I will need to re-install the operating system and applications from original media, in addition to restoring my valuable data. How you backup your computer information is up to you. The important thing is to make good backups.

Some partition editing actions inherently carry a higher risk for loss of data. In the recipes that follow we will indicate which actions have the highest risk.

Disclaimer

This book is distributed in the hope that it will be useful, but without any warranty; without even the implied warranty of merchantability or fitness for a particular purpose.

And now with the necessities out of the way, let us get on with learning how to manage our partitions.

Creating live media and running GParted (Must know)

We will need a copy of the GParted software for all of the recipes that follow. As such, we will start by downloading GParted Live, burning the image to a CD, and then booting from the CD.

Getting ready

You will need a blank CD-R or CD-R/W disc, a CD burner, and CD writing software.

How to do it...

Follow these steps to create a Live CD:

1. Download the disk image file `gparted-live-w.x.y-z.iso` for the latest stable release of GParted Live from the GParted website, `http://gparted.org/download.php`.

2. Optionally, verify the integrity of the downloaded file by running a program to determine the MD5SUM of the `.iso` file and ensuring that this value matches the MD5SUM checksum listed on the above mentioned web page.

3. Insert a blank CD and use the CD writing software to "burn" the `.iso` file to the blank CD as an image. The `.iso` file must be burned as an image. If the `.iso` file is written as data then the CD will not boot up a computer.

Now, boot your computer using the Live CD:

1. Reboot your computer with GParted Live CD in the CD tray of your computer.

2. Press the *Enter* key when the GParted Live boot screen is displayed:

3. Press the *Enter* key to use the standard US keymap:

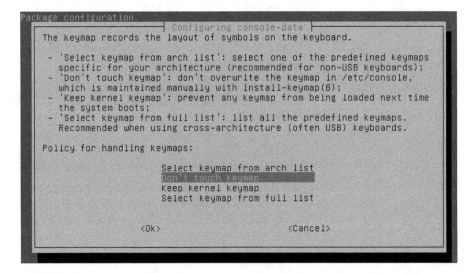

4. Press the *Enter* key to use the US English language:

```
Looking for keymap to install:
NONE
*****************************************************
Loading language settings:
 01: Bresilian           18: Latvian
 02: British English     19: Macedonian
 03: Bulgarian           20: Norwegian
 04: Catalan             21: Nepali
 05: Czech               22: Portuguese
 06: Dutch               23: Punjabi
 07: Finnish             24: Russian
 08: French              25: Spanish
 09: Galician            26: Simplified Chinese
 10: German              27: Sloven
 11: Greek               28: Swedish
 12: Hebrew              29: Traditional Chinese (Hong Kong)
 13: Hungarian           30: Traditional Chinese (Taiwan)
 14: Italian             31: Turkish
 15: Japan               32: Ukrainian
 16: Kinyarwanda         33: US English
 17: Lithuanian          34: Vietnamese

Which language do you prefer ?
[33] _
```

5. Press the *Enter* key to start up the default graphical environment:

```
 15: Japan               32: Ukrainian
 16: Kinyarwanda         33: US English
 17: Lithuanian          34: Vietnamese

Which language do you prefer ?
[33]
The default language US English is used
Language selected en_US
Setting locale in /etc/default/locale...
Setting locale in /etc/environment...
done!
*****************************************************
///NOTE/// Later we will enter graphical environment if you choose '0'. However,
 if graphical environment (X-window) fails to start, you can:
Run "sudo Forcevideo" to configure it again. Choose 1024x768, 800x600 or 640x480
 as your resolution and the driver for your VGA card, etc. Most of the time you
can accept the default values if you have no idea about them.
If failing to enter graphical environment, and it does not return to text mode,
you can reboot again, and choose '1' here to config X manually.
---------------------------------------------
Which mode do you prefer ?
(0) Continue to start X to use GParted automatically
(1) Run 'Forcevideo' to config X manually
(2) Enter command line prompt
[0] _
```

6. You are now ready to begin using GParted.

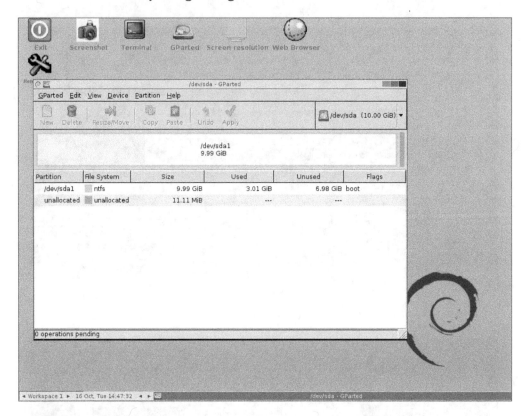

How it works...

The best way to use GParted is from Live media, such as GParted Live burned to a CD or written to a USB flash drive. When your computer is booted from the hard drive, the operating system has access to the partitions. To prevent this access and hence enable all supported partition editing actions, boot your computer using GParted Live removable media.

By downloading and using the latest stable release of GParted Live, you will have access to all the latest features and bug fixes.

There's more...

In this example we used all of the default settings for GParted Live. However, several other options are available. For example if you choose the mode to load **GParted Live** to RAM then you will have access to your CD tray, which can be useful for making data backups to CD. Other options allow you to choose a different keyboard layout or select a different language.

Missing MD5SUM

If the MD5SUM program is not available on your computer, you can locate this software on the Internet with search criteria such as `md5sum download`.

Missing CD writer software

If you do not have CD writing software, you can locate this type of software on the Internet with search criteria such as `cd burning software`.

Additional help

The GParted website contains additional resources to help you. See `http://gparted.org/help.php`.

For example, you can learn how to install GParted Live on a USB flash drive, on a hard drive, or on a PXE server.

Identifying proper disk device (Must know)

Before performing any partition editing, it is important to select the correct disk device. To do this we look at details, such as size, model, manufacturer, and device name. These details contain valuable information that will guide selection of the correct device.

How to do it...

1. Size is the first indicator of which device to choose. To select a device, go to the **GParted | Devices** menu option and select a device of the correct size.

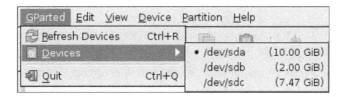

2. If there is more than one device of the same size, additional information is needed. To view more device information, select the **View | Device Information** menu option, which will toggle the display of the device information pane, as shown in the following screenshot:

```
                                    /dev/sdc1
                                    7.47 GiB
```

Device Information		Partition	File System	Label	Size	Used	Unused	Flags
Model: Patriot Memory		/dev/sdc1	fat32	Peppermint	7.47 GiB	478.75 MiB	7.00 GiB	boot, lba
Size: 7.47 GiB								
Path: /dev/sdc								
Partition table: msdos								
Heads: 247								
Sectors/track: 62								
Cylinders: 1022								
Total sectors: 15663104								
Sector size: 512								

3. Examine the device details, such as model, partition table, and sector size, to see if this is the device to modify.

4. If there are two or more identical disk drives from the same manufacturer, then look at the partition layout.

5. Examine the partitions in the graphical display area, and also in the text list of details to see if this is the correct device.

6. If there are two identical disks with the same partition layout, then this might be a RAID configuration. In this situation examine the device name as well. RAID arrays, which are configured using the motherboard BIOS, will have device names that start with /dev/mapper/. . . . With RAID configurations choose the RAID device name. Please note that the /dev/mapper directory might also contain **Logical Volume Management** (**LVM**) or encrypted (dm-crypt) entries.

    If the correct device has not yet been chosen, then go back to step 1 and start over by selecting a different device.

How it works...

Often, size alone can distinguish among different disk devices. Disk sizes can be a little tricky though because disk manufacturers use SI decimal prefixes (for example, 1 MB = 1,000,000 bytes), whereas GParted uses IEC binary prefixes (for example, 1 MiB = 1,048,576 bytes). The difference between these two methods becomes quite noticeable as the disk size becomes larger. For example, 160 GB is about 149 GiB. Hence the size of the disk device as shown in GParted will always be a lower number than the one reported by the disk manufacturer.

The device name is also useful to help distinguish among different disk devices. Device names vary by disk device as shown in the following table:

Disk device types	Sample device names
Hard disk drives (IDE, SATA, SCSI), USB flash drives, and dedicated hardware RAID drives	`/dev/sda`
	`/dev/sdb`
	`/dev/sdc`
Memory Cards (SD, SDHC, MMC)	`/dev/mmcblk0`
	`/dev/mmcblk1`
Motherboard BIOS (ATA) RAID drives	`/dev/mapper/isw_ ...`
	`/dev/mapper/nvidia_ ...`
	`/dev/mapper/jmicron_ ...`
Linux Software RAID drives	`/dev/md0`
	`/dev/md1`

 Historically IDE drives in Linux had device names such as `/dev/hda` and `/dev/hdb`. With Linux kernels >= 2.6.20 the device names became the same as for SATA, SCSI, and USB (for example, `/dev/sda`).

There's more...

There is another handy way to select a disk device. You can select a disk device from the drop-down menu in the upper-left hand corner of the window.

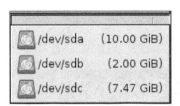

Device containing data shown as unallocated

If you know the disk device contains data, but GParted shows the entire device as unallocated then there is no need to panic. It is possible there is a problem with the partition table.

Check for partition table problems by double-clicking on the unallocated disk device. This will bring up an information window, as shown in the following screenshot, which displays possible warnings about the device:

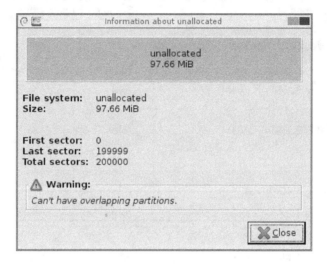

Two examples of warning messages that indicate partition table problems are as follows. A valid partition table:

- ▸ Can't have overlapping partitions
- ▸ Can't have a partition outside the disk

Resolution of these problems usually requires manually editing the partition table. The GParted website FAQ contains instructions on how to approach fixing these problems. See `http://gparted.org/faq.php`.

You can also seek help in the GParted forum. See `http://gparted.org/forum.php`.

Identifying partitions and actions available (Must know)

With the proper disk device selected, it is important to choose the correct partition. In the following steps we will discover how to identify partitions and the actions available.

Getting ready

Before picking a partition, it helps to know some background information about the primary types of file systems for each operating system. A brief summary of default file systems for operating systems is as follows:

Default File System	Operating System
EXT2/3/4	Linux
FAT16	Windows 95/NT/3.x, DOS
FAT32	Windows XP/ME/98
HFS+	Mac OS X
JFS	IBM AIX
NTFS	Windows 7/Vista/XP/2000/NT, Windows Server 2008/2003
UFS	BSD, SunOS/Solaris, HP-UX
XFS	SGI IRIX

Note that many operating systems support more than just the above listed default file systems. For example FAT16 and FAT32 are supported by many operating systems. As such, FAT16 and FAT32 are useful for sharing information between operating systems.

Typically drive letters in Windows and DOS correspond to partitions, except when the file system is not recognized by these operating systems.

With Windows and DOS, c: is often the first, and perhaps the only, partition on the disk device. Normally this partition is used in the boot process and has the **boot** flag set, as shown in the following screenshot. Note that only one partition on a disk device can have the **boot** flag set.

Partition	File System	Size	Used	Unused	Flags
/dev/sda1	ntfs	9.99 GiB	3.01 GiB	6.98 GiB	boot
unallocated	unallocated	11.11 MiB	---	---	

Many other partition layouts are possible. For example, some disk devices contain an **Original Equipment Manufacturer** (**OEM**) rescue partition at the start of the drive and hence the main operating system resides in a later partition.

How to do it...

1. Select the partition you wish to modify.

2. If the partition has a padlock icon, or key icon beside the partition entry, then the partition is in use. To be able to modify the partition, select the menu option, **Partition | Unmount**, to unmount the file system.

3. Note that Linux swap and lvm2 physical volumes will display a different menu name. Specifically:

   ❑ For linux-swap, the menu option is:

      Partition | Swapoff

   ❑ For lvm2 pv, the menu option is:

      Partition | Deactivate

Partition	File System	Mount Point
/dev/sda1	ntfs	/media/xyz
unallocated	unallocated	

4. If you wish to view the actions available for file systems, select the menu option, **View | File System Support**, which will open a window with details for the actions supported.

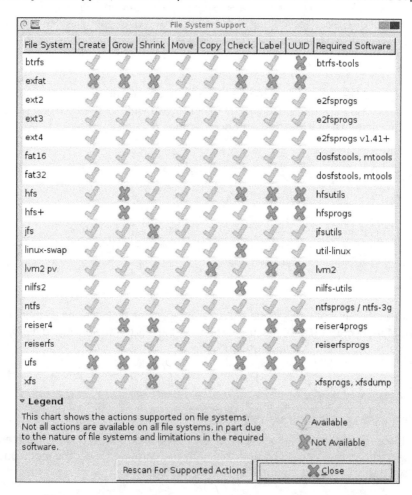

File System Support

File System	Create	Grow	Shrink	Move	Copy	Check	Label	UUID	Required Software
btrfs	✓	✓	✓	✓	✓	✓	✓	✗	btrfs-tools
exfat	✗	✗	✗	✓	✓	✗	✗	✗	
ext2	✓	✓	✓	✓	✓	✓	✓	✓	e2fsprogs
ext3	✓	✓	✓	✓	✓	✓	✓	✓	e2fsprogs
ext4	✓	✓	✓	✓	✓	✓	✓	✓	e2fsprogs v1.41+
fat16	✓	✓	✓	✓	✓	✓	✓	✓	dosfstools, mtools
fat32	✓	✓	✓	✓	✓	✓	✓	✓	dosfstools, mtools
hfs	✓	✗	✓	✓	✓	✗	✗	✗	hfsutils
hfs+	✓	✗	✓	✓	✓	✓	✗	✗	hfsprogs
jfs	✓	✓	✗	✓	✓	✓	✓	✓	jfsutils
linux-swap	✓	✓	✓	✓	✓	✗	✓	✓	util-linux
lvm2 pv	✓	✓	✓	✓	✗	✓	✗	✗	lvm2
nilfs2	✓	✓	✓	✓	✓	✗	✓	✓	nilfs-utils
ntfs	✓	✓	✓	✓	✓	✓	✓	✓	ntfsprogs / ntfs-3g
reiser4	✓	✗	✗	✓	✓	✓	✗	✗	reiser4progs
reiserfs	✓	✓	✓	✓	✓	✓	✓	✓	reiserfsprogs
ufs	✗	✗	✗	✓	✓	✗	✗	✗	
xfs	✓	✓	✗	✓	✓	✓	✓	✓	xfsprogs, xfsdump

▾ **Legend**

This chart shows the actions supported on file systems. Not all actions are available on all file systems, in part due to the nature of file systems and limitations in the required software.

✓ Available

✗ Not Available

Rescan For Supported Actions   ✗ Close

How it works...

When a partition is selected, the partition editing actions that are not available will be grayed out in the menus, and the corresponding buttons in the taskbar will be disabled.

Many partition editing actions require that the file system is not in use. Hence to be able to perform the widest range of editing actions, the file system must not be mounted, enabled as swap space, or in use in any other way.

There's more...

Operating systems, such as Linux, can use many different types of file systems and do not require the **boot** flag to be set to boot the computer.

Labeling the partitions

To make it easier to identify partitions in the future, you can set a label on the file system in the partition. The steps to set a label on a partition will be covered later under the *Formatting a partition* recipe.

Checking and repairing a partition (Should know)

Sometimes problems arise with the file systems in partitions. In the following section you will learn how to identify and address problems with file systems.

How to do it...

You can identify possible file system problems by following these steps:

1. GParted indicates possible file system problems by placing an exclamation mark triangle icon beside the partition entry. If GParted displays the exclamation mark triangle icon, as shown in the following screenshot, select the partition:

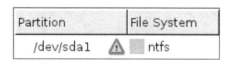

2. Choose the **Partition | Information** menu option.

3. View the problem in the **Warning** section at the bottom of the window.

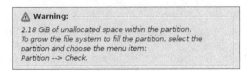

4. Click on **Close** to close the Information window.

You can attempt repair of file system problems by following these steps:

1. Choose the **Partition | Check** menu option to queue the check operation. The queued check operation is shown in the operations pane at the bottom of the window. The operations pane appears when at least one operation is queued.

2. Choose the **Edit | Apply All Operations** menu option to apply the queued operations to disk.

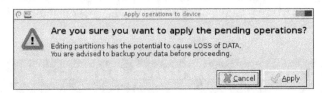

3. Click on **Apply** to apply operations to disk.

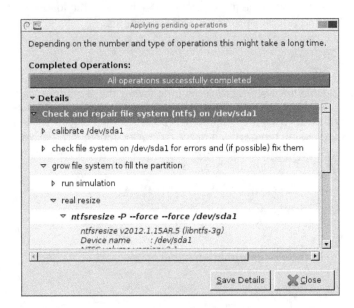

4. Click on **Close** to close the apply operations to disk window.

How it works...

When GParted reads information from the device partitions and file systems, it makes notes of any problems encountered. The presence of these problems is indicated by an exclamation mark triangle icon beside the partition entry.

Examples of problems that occur are as follows:

- The file system contains inconsistencies and requires repair
- The file system is smaller than the containing partition and could be grown to use space more effectively
- Some required software is missing from the Linux installation so GParted is unable to determine space usage in a file system

Note that the GParted Live image contains all of the required software

There's more...

While GParted operations are in the process of being applied, you can click on **Details** to open a details pane. Inside this pane you can click on each of the hierarchy of operations to expand and view more detailed information.

Checking and fixing NTFS file systems

An NTFS file system can become inconsistent if Windows is not cleanly shut down, for example, if the computer was powered off while it was running. To repair the NTFS file system, the preferred practice is to boot into Windows, open a command prompt (press Windows logo + *R* and enter `cmd.exe`) and use the check disk program by entering the following command:

```
chkdsk /f /r
```

Where the parameters indicate the following:

- `/f`: Fixes errors on the disk. The disk must be locked.
- `/r`: Locates bad sectors and recovers readable information. The disk must be locked.

Note that if `chkdsk` cannot lock the drive, a message appears that asks you if you want to check the drive the next time you restart the computer. Answer `y` to this question, as shown in the following screenshot:

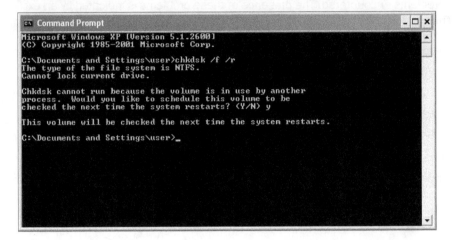

After entering the `chkdsk` command, go through two reboot cycles to ensure that Windows has completely repaired the file system. A screen similar to the following is shown while `chkdsk` is running:

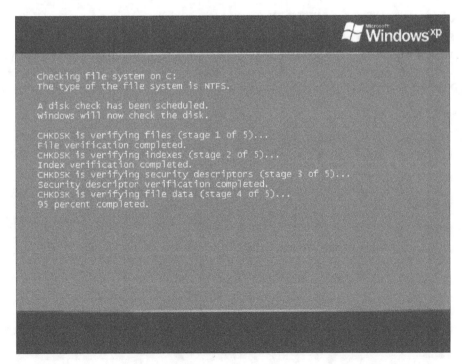

Getting space by shrinking a partition (Should know)

When a partition contains extra space it can be beneficial to free up this space for use in other partitions. This section demonstrates how to get space by shrinking a partition.

Note that the resize and move functionality is a core building block of re-organizing partitions. As shrinking, moving, and growing partitions involve different considerations and levels of risk, these three actions have been separated into their own individual tasks.

Getting ready

Before before performing this task, we highly recommend that you backup your data. This recipe involves moving the end of a partition boundary which is a moderate risk activity.

When you shrink a partition, the freed up space will be available immediately to the right of the partition. If this freed up space is required in a different location on the disk, you might need to consider moving other partitions, or resizing the start or end of the extended partition. Moving or growing partitions is covered in later tasks.

Remember that to perform operations on a partition, the partition must not be mounted or otherwise active. For operations on the extended partition, none of the logical partitions can be mounted or otherwise active. You can use the Partition menu to unmount, swapoff, or deactivate partitions as needed.

How to do it...

1. Select a partition containing unused space.

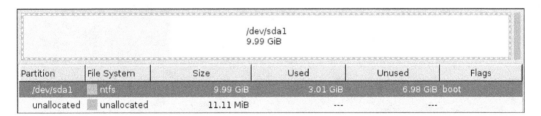

Partition	File System	Size	Used	Unused	Flags
/dev/sda1	ntfs	9.99 GiB	3.01 GiB	6.98 GiB	boot
unallocated	unallocated	11.11 MiB	---	---	

2. Choose the menu option **Partition | Resize/Move** and a **Resize/Move** window is displayed.

3. Click on the right-hand side of the partition and drag the right-hand side to the left.

> Leave at least 10 percent or more unused space in the partition because many file systems require some unused space to be able to function properly.

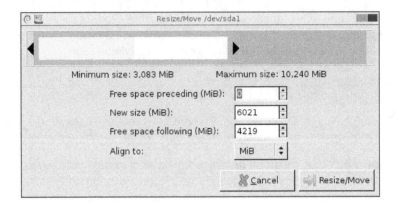

4. Click on **Resize/Move** to queue the shrink operation. The queued shrink operation is shown in the operations pane.

5. Choose the menu option **Edit | Apply All Operations** to apply the queued operations to disk.

6. Click on **Apply** to apply operations to disk.

7. Click on **Close** to close the apply operations to disk window.

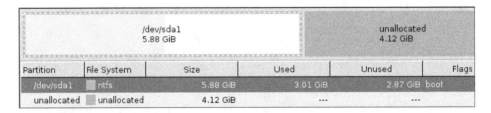

How it works...

In the above steps, we moved the right-hand side of the partition, also known as the end of the partition. This instructs GParted to resize (shrink) the partition.

In this example, we left many options at the default values. If you wish to maintain compatibility with old operating systems, such as DOS, then you should set the **Align to** drop down list to the **Cylinder** setting. To ensure optimum space usage it is best to use the same alignment setting for all partitions on a disk device, normally MiB alignment with modern operating systems.

If you require more precise partition sizing, you can enter values or use the arrows in the **New size**, or **Free space following** spin boxes.

There's more...

If you resize a partition containing an NTFS file system, you should reboot into Windows twice. This permits Windows to perform file system consistency checks.

Moving the left-hand side of a partition

If the left-hand side of the partition, also known as the beginning of the partition, is moved, the operation is no longer simply a partition resize. Two steps are required due to the metadata contained at the beginning of the file system. One operation is needed to shrink the partition, and another to move the partition.

Moving the start of a partition involves extra considerations that will be discussed later in the *Moving a partition* recipe.

Creating a new partition (Should know)

In this recipe we will cover the steps to create a new partition for storing data. We also discuss options for creating different types of partitions.

How to do it...

1. Select unallocated space on a disk device.

Partition	File System	Size	Used	Unused	Flags
/dev/sda1	ntfs	5.88 GiB	3.01 GiB	2.87 GiB	boot
unallocated	unallocated	4.12 GiB	---	---	

2. Choose the **Partition | New** menu option and a new partition window is displayed.

3. Optionally, you can set the partition **New size** to a smaller value.

> To adjust the partition size click on one of the side arrows on the partition graphic (shown in the following screenshot) and drag it to left or right. Alternatively enter a new value for **New Size** or click on the up and down spin button arrows beside the number.
>
> To move the entire partition click on the partition and drag it to left or right.

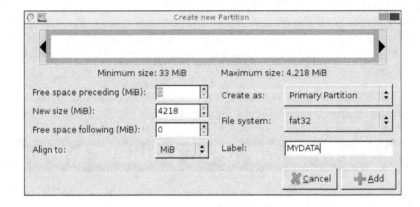

4. Select a **File system** for the partition; for example, **fat32**. A list of default file systems used by operating systems can be found in the *Identifying partitions and actions available* recipe.

5. Enter a **Label** for the file system; for example, MYDATA.

6. Click on **Add**.

7. Choose the **Edit | Apply All Operations** menu option to apply the queued operations to disk.

8. Click on **Apply** to apply operations to disk.

9. Click on **Close** to close the apply operations to disk window:

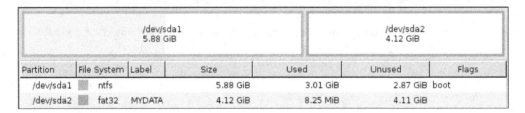

How it works...

The above steps instruct GParted to create a partition using all of the unallocated space. Further, the partition is formatted with a file system with the label specified (for example, MYDATA).

We left many options at the default values. Some other things to consider are:

- ▸ Creating the partition as a different type. For example, with an MSDOS partition table you might try using **Create as** an **Extended Partition**, or **Create as** a **Logical Partition**. Read on to learn why you might want to use different partition types.

- ▸ Setting the **Align to** drop-down list to **Cylinder** setting if you wish to maintain compatibility with older operating systems, such as DOS.

There's more...

One of the most common partition tables in use is the MSDOS partition table. This partition table has a limitation of four partition slots. The four slots can consist of up to four primary partitions, or up to three primary partitions and one extended partition. The extended partition is a special type of partition that can contain multiple logical partitions. If you wish to have more than four partitions in an MSDOS partition table, you need to create one extended partition. Inside the extended partition you can create more than one logical partition.

The choice of partition type is important because after a partition has been created, the partition type cannot be easily changed. For example, a primary partition cannot be easily turned into a logical partition, or vice versa. To change the partition type the partition must be deleted.

The three partition types use device numbers in the device name as follows:

- ▸ Primary partitions use device numbers 1 through 4 (for example, /dev/sda3).
- ▸ An extended partition uses one of the device numbers from 1 through 4.
- ▸ Logical partitions use device numbers 5 and higher (for example, /dev/sda12).

Note that only one extended partition is permitted in an MSDOS partition table.

The following diagram depicts a primary partition (sda1), followed by an extended partition (sda2), which contains three logical partitions (sda5, sda6, and sda7).

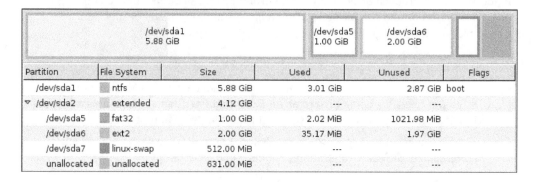

Partition	File System	Size	Used	Unused	Flags
/dev/sda1	ntfs	5.88 GiB	3.01 GiB	2.87 GiB	boot
▽ /dev/sda2	extended	4.12 GiB	---	---	
/dev/sda5	fat32	1.00 GiB	2.02 MiB	1021.98 MiB	
/dev/sda6	ext2	2.00 GiB	35.17 MiB	1.97 GiB	
/dev/sda7	linux-swap	512.00 MiB	---	---	
unallocated	unallocated	631.00 MiB	---	---	

The extended and logical partitions in this example were set up by first creating the extended partition sda2. Then, within the extended partition we created the logical partitions sda5, sda6, and sda7.

Managing partition flags

Most computer users will not need to be concerned about setting partition flags. However, for users configuring more complex storage scenarios, such as RAID or **Logical Volume Management** (**LVM**), the following steps demonstrate how to toggle partition flags to be set or unset.

1. Select an existing partition; for example, a partition that has already been created.

2. Choose the **Partition | Manage Flags** menu option and a **Manage flags** window will be displayed.

3. As shown in the following screenshot, select the checkbox to toggle the flag between set and unset (for example, **lvm**)

4. Click on **Close** and the flag will be set or unset as you indicated.

Moving a partition (Become an expert)

Moving a partition is a complex and long running operation. As there are implications to moving a partition, we will discuss these along with the steps to move a partition.

Getting ready

Before performing this task, we highly recommend that you backup your data. This task involves moving the start of a partition boundary, which is a high-risk activity.

One implication of moving a system partition is possibly breaking the boot process. The boot process can be repaired, so before moving a partition you should be prepared to repair the boot configuration. Specifically, you will need your operating system install media, and to be ready to check the GParted website for details on how to repair the boot process.

How to do it...

1. Select a partition to move.

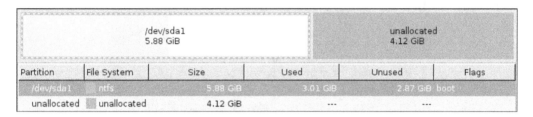

Partition	File System	Size	Used	Unused	Flags
/dev/sda1	ntfs	5.88 GiB	3.01 GiB	2.87 GiB	boot
unallocated	unallocated	4.12 GiB	---	---	

2. Choose the **Partition | Resize/Move** menu option and a **Resize/Move** window will be displayed:

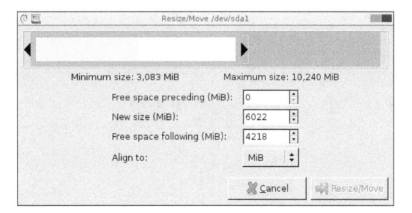

3. Click in the middle of the partition and drag the partition in the direction you want to move. (for example, to the right). Note that if grow and/or shrink are supported for the file system then you can also change the size of the partition.

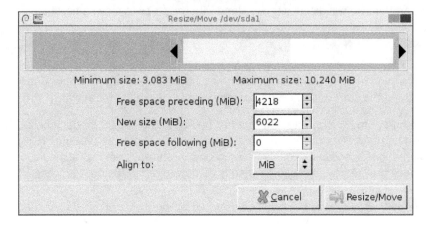

4. Click on **Resize/Move** to queue the move operation.

5. Click on **OK** to acknowledge the warning.

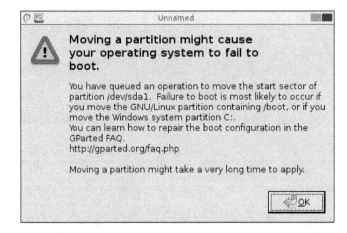

6. Choose the menu option **Edit | Apply All Operations** to apply the queued operations to disk.

7. Click on **Apply** to apply operations to disk.

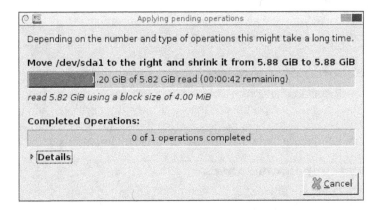

8. Click on **Close** to close the apply operations to disk window.

Partition	File System	Size	Used	Unused	Flags
unallocated	unallocated	4.12 GiB	---	---	
/dev/sda1	ntfs	5.88 GiB	3.01 GiB	2.87 GiB	boot

How it works...

Before moving a partition, GParted reads all sectors to check for bad sectors. After a successful read of all sectors, GParted will begin copying sectors to their new location. This process can take a very long time since many sector read and write actions are required.

The move process is different for an extended partition. Since an extended partition is a container for logical partitions, it does not have its own file system. As such, moving an extended partition involves moving the partition boundaries only.

Moving can be combined with resizing a partition. Since the move operation is distinct from the resize operation, GParted will optimally determine the order of the resize and move steps to minimize the amount of data to be moved.

In this example, we left many options at the default values. If you wish to maintain compatibility with old operating systems, such as DOS, then you should set the **Align to** drop down list to the **Cylinder** setting.

If you require more precise partition movement, you can type in values or use the arrows in the **Free space preceding**, **New size**, or **Free space following** spin boxes.

There's more...

If you resize a partition containing an NTFS file system, you should reboot into Windows twice. This permits Windows to perform file system consistency checks.

Booting problems after moving

The configuration for boot loaders often includes data on specific disk locations in order to boot an operating system. If a partition is involved in the boot process, and the partition is moved then this can break the boot process. When the boot process is broken, the boot configuration must be repaired. A brief summary of repair commands is in the next section.

Windows 7/Vista repair commands

The following commands are entered at the command line when using the Recovery Console from the Windows Vista or Windows 7 installation disk.

▸ To repair the Master Boot Record of the boot disk:

```
bootrec /fixmbr
```

▸ To write a new partition boot sector to the system partition:

```
bootrec /fixboot
```

▸ To rebuild the **Boot Configuration Data** (**BCD**) store:

```
bootrec /rebuildbcd
```

Windows XP repair commands

The following commands are entered at the command line when using the Recovery Console from the Windows XP installation disk.

▸ To repair the Master Boot Record of the boot disk:

```
fixmbr
```

▸ To write a new partition boot sector to the system partition:

```
fixboot
```

▸ To rebuild the boot.ini configuration file:

```
bootcfg /rebuild
```

For more information about repairing the boot process for some common boot loaders, refer to the GParted website frequently asked questions page. See `http://gparted.org/faq.php`.

Adding space by growing a partition (Should know)

When a partition is running out of free space it can be useful to add more space to the partition. Adding space is possible if unallocated space is available, or can be made available, immediately adjacent to the partition. In this recipe we cover the steps to add space to a partition.

Getting ready

Before performing this task, we highly recommend that you backup your data. This task involves moving the end of a partition boundary which is a moderate risk activity.

Note that in order to perform actions on a partition, the partition must be unmounted. In the case of an extended partition, all of the logical partitions must be unmounted or otherwise inactive.

If there is no unallocated space immediately adjacent to the partition you wish to grow, then you might need to shrink, move, or delete other partitions to free up adjacent unallocated space.

The location of the unallocated space is important. To add space to a primary partition the unallocated space must be outside of the extended partition. To add space to a logical partition the unallocated space must be within the extended partition. Hence you might need to resize the extended partition, placing the unallocated space outside or inside the extended partition.

How to do it...

1. Select the partition to add space to.

Partition	File System	Size	Used	Unused	Flags
/dev/sda1	ntfs	5.88 GiB	5.58 GiB	308.10 MiB	boot
unallocated	unallocated	4.12 GiB	---	---	

2. Choose the **Partition | Resize/Move** menu option and a **Resize/Move** window is displayed:

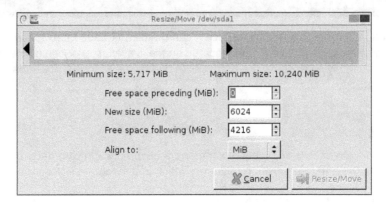

3. Click on the right-hand side of the partition and drag it to the right.

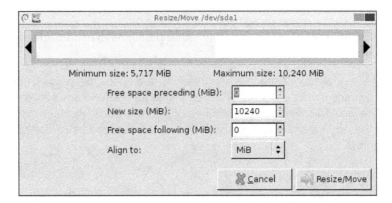

4. Click on **Resize/Move** to queue the grow operation. The queued grow operation is shown in the operations pane.

5. Choose the **Edit | Apply All Operations** menu option to apply the queued operations to disk.

6. Click on **Apply** to apply operations to disk.

7. Click on **Close** to close the apply operations to disk window.

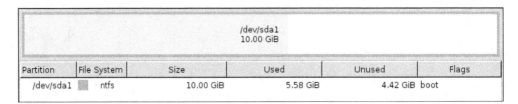

How it works...

In the above steps, we expanded the right-hand side of the partition, also known as the end of the partition. This instructs GParted to resize (grow) the partition.

In this example, we left many options at the default values. If you wish to maintain compatibility with old operating systems, such as DOS, you should set the **Align to** drop down list to the **Cylinder** setting. If you require more precise partition sizing, you can enter values or use the arrows in the for **New size**, or **Free space following** spin boxes.

There's more...

If you resize a partition containing an NTFS file system, you should reboot into Windows twice. This permits Windows to perform file system consistency checks.

Moving the left-hand side of a partition

If the left-hand side of the partition, also known as the beginning of the partition, is moved then the operation is no longer simply a partition resize. Two steps are required due to the metadata contained at the beginning of the file system. One operation is needed to move the partition, and another to grow the partition.

Moving the start of a partition involves extra considerations that are discussed earlier in the *Moving a partition* recipe.

Formatting a partition (Should know)

Normally you choose the file system type when creating a new partition. However, sometimes you want to keep an existing partition location exactly the same, but format it with a new file system so you can use the partition for a different purpose. The following steps describe how to accomplish this task.

Getting ready

As formatting a partition will overwrite the existing data, if you wish to keep the data you must first make a backup.

How to do it...

1. Select the partition to format:

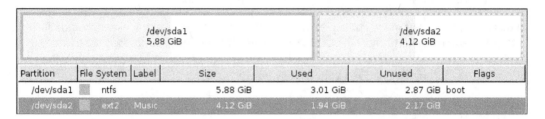

Partition	File System	Label	Size	Used	Unused	Flags
/dev/sda1	ntfs		5.88 GiB	3.01 GiB	2.87 GiB	boot
/dev/sda2	ext2	Music	4.12 GiB	1.94 GiB	2.17 GiB	

2. Choose the **Partition | Format** menu option and select a file system; for example, **fat32**.

 A list of default file systems used by operating systems can be found in the *Identifying partitions and actions available* recipe.

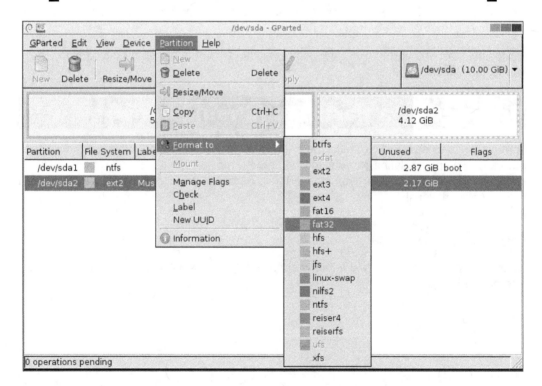

3. Choose the **Edit | Apply All Operations** menu option to apply the queued operations to disk.

4. Click on **Apply** to apply operations to disk.

5. Click on **Close** to close the apply operations to disk window.

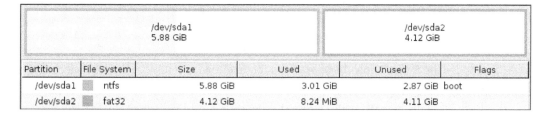

How it works...

By selecting an existing partition and choosing format, you maintain the existing partition boundaries and the partition number. The process of formatting writes new file system metadata to the partition, which destroys the links to previously existing files. Often software recovery tools can be used to recover this data, but for our purposes all data in the partition is lost.

There's more...

Formatting the partition with a new file system will overwrite the label and UUID used by the previous file system. The next two sections cover how to set a new label, and also the implications of the UUID change.

Labeling the partition

After formatting a partition you can choose to place a label on the file system to make it easier to identify the partition. You can also label other existing partitions too.

1. Select the partition to label.

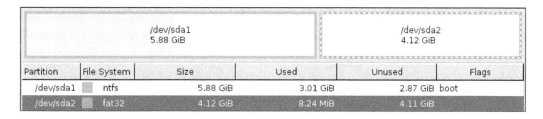

2. Choose the **Partition | Label** menu option and a **Set partition label** window is displayed.

3. Enter a **Label** for the file system; for example, `MUSIC`.

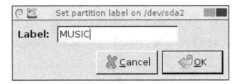

4. Click on **OK**.
5. Choose the **Edit | Apply All Operations** menu option to apply the queued operations to disk.
6. Click on **Apply** to apply operations to disk.
7. Click on **Close** to close the apply operations to disk window.

| | | | | /dev/sda1 5.88 GiB | | | /dev/sda2 4.12 GiB | |

Partition	File System	Label	Size	Used	Unused	Flags
/dev/sda1	ntfs		5.88 GiB	3.01 GiB	2.87 GiB	boot
/dev/sda2	fat32	MUSIC	4.12 GiB	8.24 MiB	4.11 GiB	

Formatting creates a new UUID

Formatting an existing partition with a new file system results in the creation of a new **Universally Unique Identifier** (**UUID**) for the file system. Additionally, the previous volume label on the file system is lost. As the UUID or volume label is often used to identify the partition, this can impact how the operating system treats the file system.

For example, in Linux, if the file system was previously automatically mounted, then it might cease to be mounted due to the change in UUID or volume label. To address this situation you might need to update configuration files, such as `/etc/fstab`, to reflect the new UUID or volume label.

For file systems recognized by Windows (ntfs, fat16, and fat32), Windows will reuse the drive letter for the new file system and UUID. For example if `G:` was used for an NTFS partition, then after you reformat the partition with fat32 Windows will reuse `G:` as the drive letter. For file systems not recognized by Windows, no drive letter is assigned.

If you need to change the Windows drive letter assignments, use the Disk Management tool. In Windows, start the Disk Management tool from the Start menu's **Run** box or from a command prompt window by entering `diskmgmt.msc`. To access the drive letter change feature, right-click on the partition that you want to assign a new drive letter to. Next, click on Change Drive Letters and Paths, and then assign an available drive letter.

Preparing a new disk device for use (Become an expert)

Often, a brand new disk device has no partition table. In this recipe we will write a partition table to the disk device. A partition table is required to be able to divide a disk device into distinct areas known as partitions.

Getting ready

Connect a new disk device to your computer.

If you wish to write a new partition table to an existing device, be sure to first backup the data on the device because you will lose the partitions and the data.

For disk devices larger than 2 TB, you should consider using gpt instead of the default msdos partition table. More information on gpt and msdos partition tables can be found later in this recipe.

How to do it...

1. Select the new disk device using the **Gparted** | **Devices** | **[your-new-disk-device]** menu option and the new device is displayed in the main window:

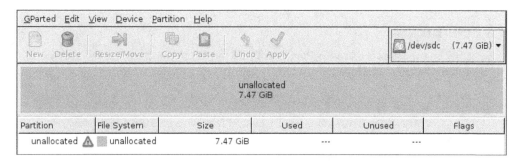

2. Check to see that the new device is shown as entirely unallocated, and check under the **Partition** column for an exclamation mark inside a triangle beside **unallocated**.

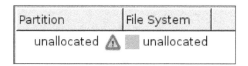

3. Double-click on the **unallocated** disk device to display **Information about unallocated**:

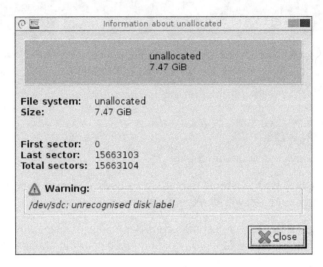

4. Confirm that the warning message reads **unrecognised disk label** to ensure that the disk device does not contain an existing partition table, also known as a disk label.

 This check helps to avoid accidentally overwriting an existing partition table and hence erasing all the partitions and data on the disk device.

5. Click on **Close.**

6. Choose the **Device | Create Partition Table** menu option and a **Create partition table** window is displayed:

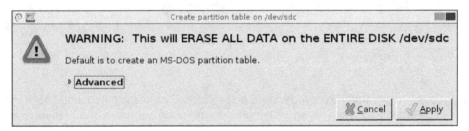

7. Optionally, click on **Advanced** and select a different type of partition table, such as **gpt**:

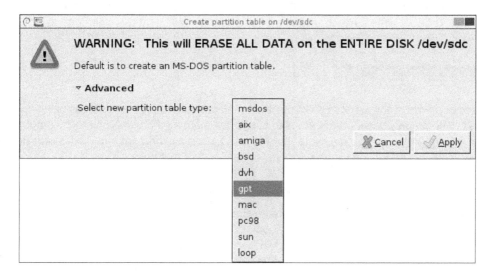

8. Click on **Apply** to write the partition table to the disk device.

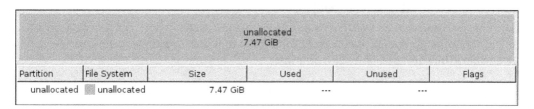

9. Choose the **View | Device Information** menu option to toggle on the device information panel display:

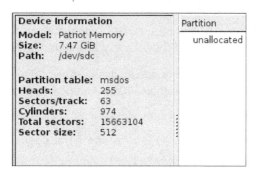

10. Confirm that the **Partition table** is the type you selected (for example, **msdos** or **gpt**).

How it works...

In this example we confirm that the disk device is missing a partition table, also known as a disk label. Then we write a new partition table to the disk device. At this point the disk device is now ready for new partitions to be created.

There's more...

GParted supports many more types of partition tables. While the gpt and msdos partition tables are commonly used, others are also supported such as mac for MacIntosh computers, and amiga for Amiga computers. Note that Mac OS X uses a hybrid gpt and msdos partition table which is described later in the appendix at the end of this book.

MSDOS partition table 2 tebibyte limit

On devices with a 512 byte sector size, the maximum size of a partition in an MSDOS partition table is about 2 tebibytes (2,199,023,255,040 bytes, or one sector less than 2 TiB). The partition must also start within the first 2 tebibytes of the disk device. Hence if you have a larger disk device, you will need to use a different partition table, such as a **GUID Partition Table** (**GPT**), to be able to access the all of the available disk space.

Booting from GPT disk device

Operating systems such as GNU/Linux and Mac OS X are able to boot from disk devices with GPT on **Personal Computer/Basic Input Output System** (**PC/BIOS**) hardware and newer **Extensible Firmware Interface** (**EFI**) firmware.

Only the newer 64-bit Windows Vista SP1, Windows 7, Windows Server 2008, and higher can boot from disk devices with GPT on newer EFI firmware. Other versions of Windows, including 32-bit versions, cannot boot from a GPT Disk and must boot from an MSDOS partition table on PC/BIOS hardware.

References

The partition table name mdsos dates back to 1983 when support for partitioned media was introduced with IBM PC DOS 2.0. IBM PC DOS was a rebranded version of Microsoft MS DOS.

For more information on disk partitioning, the msdos partition table—also known as **Master Boot Record** (**MBR**), the GUID partition table, PC/BIOS, and EFI, see:

- ▶ http://en.wikipedia.org/wiki/Disk_partitioning
- ▶ http://en.wikipedia.org/wiki/Master_boot_record
- ▶ http://en.wikipedia.org/wiki/GUID_Partition_Table
- ▶ http://en.wikipedia.org/wiki/BIOS
- ▶ http://en.wikipedia.org/wiki/Extensible_Firmware_Interface

Copying a partition (Become an expert)

Copying a partition can be a complex and long running operation. As there are implications to copying a partition, we discuss these along with the steps to copy a partition.

How to do it...

1. Select the source partition to copy:

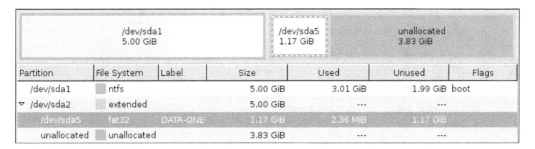

2. Choose the **Partition | Copy** menu option to place a copy of the partition in the copy buffer.

3. Optionally, if the destination device is different from the source device then select the destination disk device by choosing the **GParted | Devices | [your-destination-disk-device]** menu option, and the disk device is displayed in the main window.

4. Select unallocated space for the destination. The destination must be equal or greater in size than the source partition.

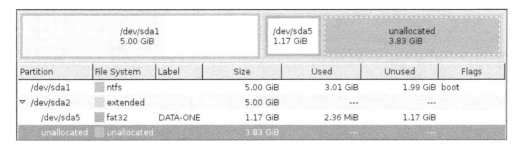

5. Choose the **Partition | Paste** menu option and a **Paste** window is displayed:

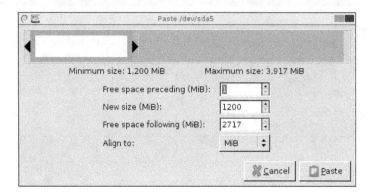

6. Click on **Paste** to queue an operation to copy the partition.

7. Choose the **Edit | Apply All Operations** menu option to apply the queued operations to disk.

8. Click on **Apply** to apply operations to disk:

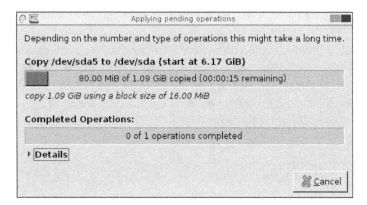

9. Click on **Close** to close the apply operations to disk window.

10. Select the copy of the partition.

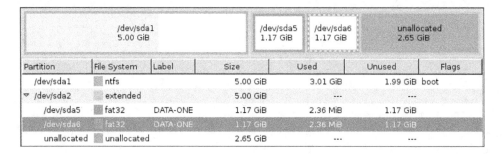

Partition	File System	Label	Size	Used	Unused	Flags
/dev/sda1	ntfs		5.00 GiB	3.01 GiB	1.99 GiB	boot
▽ /dev/sda2	extended		5.00 GiB	---	---	
/dev/sda5	fat32	DATA-ONE	1.17 GiB	2.36 MiB	1.17 GiB	
/dev/sda6	fat32	DATA-ONE	1.17 GiB	2.36 MiB	1.17 GiB	
unallocated	unallocated		2.65 GiB	---	---	

11. Choose the **Partition | New UUID** menu option to queue an operation to set a new **Universally Unique Identifier** (**UUID**) on the file system.

12. If the source file file system is NTFS or FAT then a warning will be displayed. Click on **OK** to acknowledge the warning.

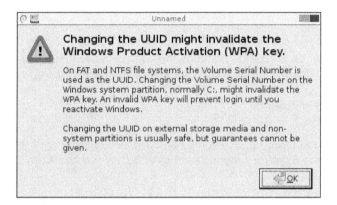

13. Select the copy of the partition.

14. Choose the **Partition | Label** menu option and a **Set partition label** window is displayed.

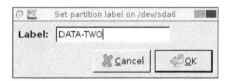

15. Enter a new **label** different from the source partition; for example, DATA-TWO.

16. Click on **OK**.

17. Choose the **Edit | Apply All Operations** menu option to apply the queued operations to disk.

18. Click on **Apply** to apply operations to disk.

19. Click on **Close** to close the apply operations to disk window.

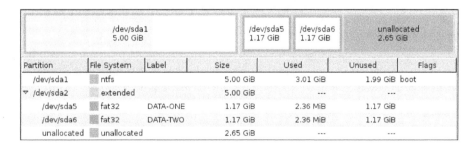

How it works...

GParted performs copy operations either by using file system tools or by copying sector by sector. For file systems such as NTFS and XFS, GParted uses native file system tools to perform the copy. For file systems lacking native file system copy tools, GParted performs a sector by sector copy.

The copied partition has the same UUID and label as the source partition. These duplicate UUIDs and labels can cause grief to operating systems because these values are supposed to be unique. To avoid such problems this task sets a new UUID and changes the label.

There's more...

In this example, we left many options at the default values. If you wish to maintain compatibility with old operating systems, such as DOS, then set the **Align to** drop down list to the **Cylinder** setting.

If you require more precise partition sizing, you can enter values or use the arrows in the **Free space preceding**, **New size**, or **Free space following** spin boxes. Note that the destination partition size can be set larger than the source partition. For XFS file systems only, the destination partition can be set smaller than the source partition.

UUID and Windows Product Activation

The UUID in the Windows system partition (normally C: drive) is used in the Windows Product Activation (WPA) scheme. Changes to this UUID might invalidate the WPA key. An invalid WPA key prevents login until you reactivate Windows. As such, if you change the UUID in the Windows system partition, you should be prepared to reactivate Windows.

Copying a partition for backup

If you copy a partition for the purpose of a backup, you will want the partition to be an exact copy (for example, the same UUID and label).

The steps to make a backup copy are first to connect the backup disk device. Then perform the copy operation steps as listed above, but skip steps 10 and higher. After you finish using GParted, shut down your computer and remove the backup disk device. Failure to remove the backup disk device may cause confusion due to duplicate UUIDs or duplicate labels.

Pasting into existing partition

Pasting into an existing partition is useful when restoring a partition from backup. To do this, select an existing partition as the destination. This overwrites all the data in the existing partition, so if you need any of this data then be sure to make a backup prior to applying the paste operation.

Copying all partitions

GParted can be used to copy all partitions on one disk device to another disk device. The process must be performed one partition at a time. If the destination disk is smaller, you might consider shrinking partitions with free space prior to copying the partitions.

GParted does not copy the boot code needed to start an operating system. To boot from the destination disk device, you will need to restore the boot process. To learn how to restore the boot process, see the earlier recipe, *Moving a partition*.

Deleting a partition (Should know)

Deleting a partition will free up space, enabling you to use the space in other new or existing partitions. This recipe covers the steps to delete a partition and describes a boot problem that might arise.

Getting ready

When you delete a partition you lose all of the data inside the partition. Hence, if you need any of the data, be sure to make a backup before deleting the partition.

How to do it...

1. Select a partition to delete:

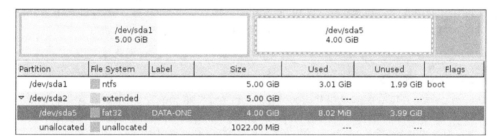

2. Choose the **Partition | Delete** menu option.
3. Choose the **Edit | Apply All Operation** menu option to apply the queued operations to disk.
4. Click on **Apply** to apply operations to disk.

5. Click on **Close** to close the apply operations to disk window.

Partition	File System	Size	Used	Unused	Flags
/dev/sda1	ntfs	5.00 GiB	3.01 GiB	1.99 GiB	boot
▽ /dev/sda2	extended	5.00 GiB	---	---	
unallocated	unallocated	5.00 GiB	---	---	

How it works...

Deleting a primary or extended partition removes the partition entry from the partition table.

Deleting a logical partition is different. Logical partitions are a special case because each logical partition has an **Extended Boot Record** (**EBR**) associated with the partition. The EBR is used to track the partition boundaries, and also to link to the next logical partition. Due to this linking nature, deleting a logical partition affects the device names of all higher numbered logical partitions. For example, if logical partition sda5 is deleted, then logical partitions sda6 and higher will have their partition number reduced by one (for example, sda6 will become sda5).

Changes in logical partition device names can adversely affect operating system boot process. As Windows can only be installed in a primary partition, the Windows boot process will not be affected. However, for operating systems that do permit booting from a logical partition, such as GNU/Linux, you might need to edit configuration files such as /etc/fstab, or other specific boot loader configuration files to restore the ability to boot.

There's more...

Deleting a partition that is part of the boot process, such as the C: drive or a system reserved partition in Windows, might cause a computer to fail to boot. If your intention was to remove only one operating system, such as Windows, you might be surprised to find your other operating systems also fail to boot. If this occurs you should be able to restore the ability to boot using the original operating system install media.

The GParted website contains additional resources to help you restore the operating system boot. See http://gparted.org/faq.php.

Deleting a partition by accident

If you have recently deleted a partition and have not yet used this space, then there is a chance you can recover the data or restore the partition.

Data rescue steps are covered later in the *Rescuing data from a lost partition* recipe.

Moving space between partitions (Become an expert)

It can be frustrating to run out of free space in one partition (for example, `C:`) when another partition (for example, `D:`) has plenty. In this recipe we cover the steps to migrate free space from one partition to another.

Getting ready

Before before performing this task, we highly recommend that you backup your data. This task involves moving the start of a partition boundary, which is a high risk activity.

How to do it...

1. Select the partition with plenty of free space.

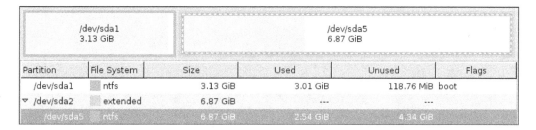

Partition	File System	Size	Used	Unused	Flags
/dev/sda1	ntfs	3.13 GiB	3.01 GiB	118.76 MiB	boot
▽ /dev/sda2	extended	6.87 GiB	---	---	
/dev/sda5	ntfs	6.87 GiB	2.54 GiB	4.34 GiB	

2. Choose the **Partition | Resize/Move** menu option and a **Resize/Move** window is displayed.

3. Click on the left-hand side of the partition and drag it to the right so that the free space is reduced by half.

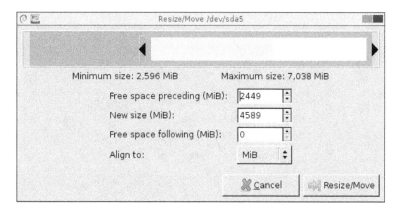

4. Click on **Resize/Move** to queue the operation.

5. Click on **OK** to acknowledge the move partition warning.

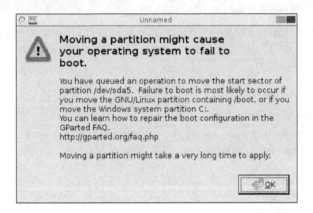

6. Select the extended partition.

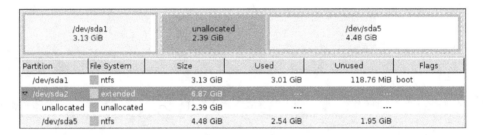

7. Choose the **Partition | Resize/Move** menu option and a **Resize/Move** window is displayed.

8. Click on the left-hand side of the partition and drag it to the right so that there is no space between the outer extended partition boundary and the inner logical partition boundary.

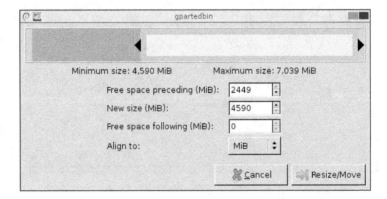

9. Click on **Resize/Move** to queue the operation.

10. Select the partition that needs more free space:

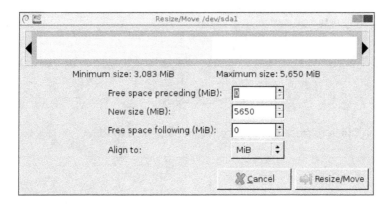

11. Choose the **Partition | Resize/Move** menu option and a **Resize/Move** window is displayed.

12. Click on the right-hand side of the partition and drag it as far to the right as possible:

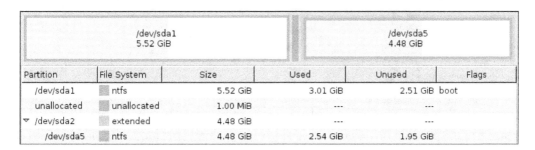

13. Click **Resize/Move** to queue the operation:

Partition	File System	Size	Used	Unused	Flags
/dev/sda1	ntfs	5.52 GiB	3.01 GiB	2.51 GiB	boot
unallocated	unallocated	1.00 MiB	---	---	
▽ /dev/sda2	extended	4.48 GiB	---	---	
/dev/sda5	ntfs	4.48 GiB	2.54 GiB	1.95 GiB	

Notice the unallocated space between sda1 and sda2. This gap, which can be up to about 8 MiB, occurs due to having cylinder aligned and MiB aligned partitions on the same disk device. In this example, the sda1 partition was created with cylinder alignment to demonstrate this potential gap.

14. Choose the **Edit | Apply All Operations** menu option to apply the queued operations, to disk.

15. Click on **Apply** to apply operations to disk.

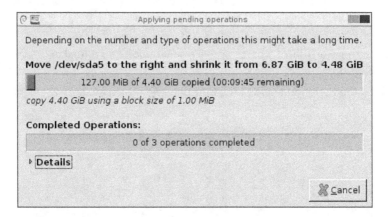

16. Click on **Close** to close the apply operations to disk window.

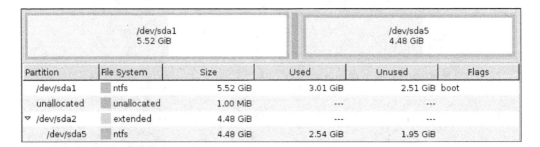

Partition	File System	Size	Used	Unused	Flags
/dev/sda1	ntfs	5.52 GiB	3.01 GiB	2.51 GiB	boot
unallocated	unallocated	1.00 MiB	---	---	
▽ /dev/sda2	extended	4.48 GiB	---	---	
/dev/sda5	ntfs	4.48 GiB	2.54 GiB	1.95 GiB	

How it works...

In order to add space to a partition, unallocated space must be available immediately adjacent to the partition. To free up this space, we use many of the recipes covered earlier.

First, we made unallocated space available by shrinking the logical partition where free space was available. Because the free space came from a logical partition inside an extended partition, and we needed to add the space to a primary partition, we had to edit three partitions to achieve the desired goal.

There's more...

As mentioned in previous recipes, if you resize or move a partition containing an NTFS file system, then you should reboot into Windows twice to permit Windows to perform file system consistency checks.

Growing or moving a partition

To grow or move a partition, unallocated space must be available adjacent to the partition:

- ▶ When growing a logical partition, the unallocated space must be within the extended partition.
- ▶ When growing a primary partition, the unallocated space must not be within the extended partition.

You can move unallocated space inside or outside of an extended partition by resizing the extended partition boundaries.

Preparing for dual boot with GNU/Linux (Become an expert)

In this recipe we pre-create partitions for the GNU/Linux operating system, the virtual memory swap space, and data sharing.

Getting ready

Before performing this task, we highly recommend that you backup your data. This task involves moving the end of a partition boundary, which is a moderate risk activity.

How to do it...

1. Select the current operating system primary partition.

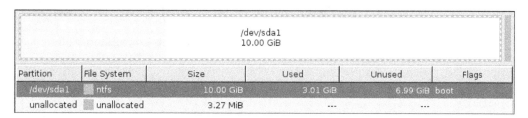

Partition	File System	Size	Used	Unused	Flags
/dev/sda1	ntfs	10.00 GiB	3.01 GiB	6.99 GiB	boot
unallocated	unallocated	3.27 MiB	---	---	

2. Choose the **Partition** | **Resize/Move** menu option and a **Resize/Move** window is displayed

3. Click on the right-hand side of the partition and drag it to the left so that at least 10 percent free space remains in the partition.

> The 10 percent figure is a safe minimum to ensure that Windows runs properly. We need to balance the space allocated to Windows with the amount of space desired for a GNU/Linux installation (OS and swap space) plus a shared data partition. For example, with Ubuntu 12.04, the absolute minimum hard disk space needed for the operating system is 500 MB.

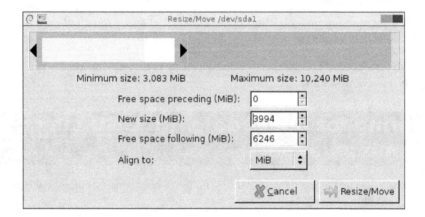

4. Click on **Resize/Move** to queue the operation.
5. Select the unallocated space.

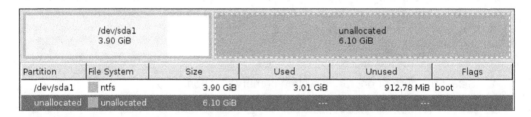

Partition	File System	Size	Used	Unused	Flags
/dev/sda1	ntfs	3.90 GiB	3.01 GiB	912.78 MiB	boot
unallocated	unallocated	6.10 GiB	---	---	

6. Choose the **Partition | New** menu option and a **Create new partition** window is displayed.

7. Click on the right hand side of the partition and drag it to the left so that the partition is bigger than the minimum size required by the GNU/Linux distribution, but leaves some space for swap (for example, twice the RAM memory size) and data partitions (for example, any space left over).

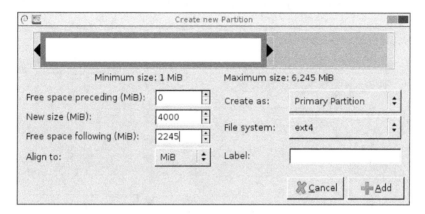

8. Click on the **File system** drop down list and select **ext4**.

 The ext4 file system is commonly used by many modern GNU/Linux distributions.

9. Click on **Add** to queue the operation.
10. Select the unallocated space.

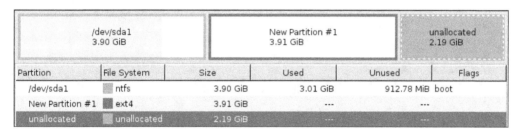

Partition	File System	Size	Used	Unused	Flags
/dev/sda1	ntfs	3.90 GiB	3.01 GiB	912.78 MiB	boot
New Partition #1	ext4	3.91 GiB	---	---	
unallocated	unallocated	2.19 GiB	---	---	

11. Choose the **Partition | New** menu option and a **Create new partition** window is displayed.

12. Click on the **Create as** drop down list and select **Extended Partition**.

 At least one extended partition is needed because an msdos partition table does not permit more than 3 primary partitions and 1 extended partition. Inside the extended partition we can create multiple logical partitions.

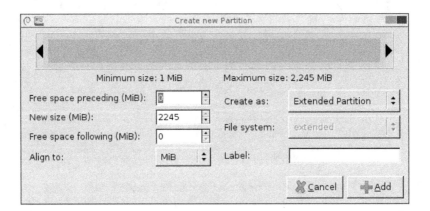

13. Click on **Add** to queue the operation.

14. Select the unallocated space from the extended partition.

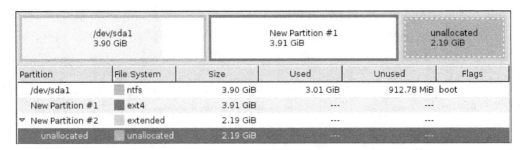

Partition	File System	Size	Used	Unused	Flags
/dev/sda1	ntfs	3.90 GiB	3.01 GiB	912.78 MiB	boot
New Partition #1	ext4	3.91 GiB	---	---	
▽ New Partition #2	extended	2.19 GiB	---	---	
unallocated	unallocated	2.19 GiB	---	---	

15. Choose the **Partition | New** menu option and a **Create new partition** window is displayed.

16. Click on the right-hand side of the partition and drag it to the left so that the new size is twice the amount of RAM in your computer (for example, 2 * 256 MiB = 512 MiB).

 A value larger than the amount of RAM will enable the use of hibernation on devices such as laptop computers.

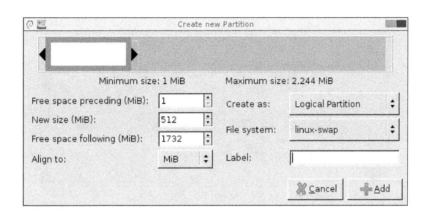

17. Click on the **File system** drop down list and select **linux-swap**.

18. Click **Add** to queue the operation.

19. Select the unallocated space from the extended partition:

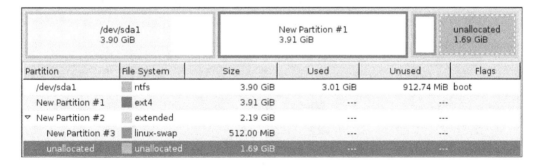

Partition	File System	Size	Used	Unused	Flags
/dev/sda1	ntfs	3.90 GiB	3.01 GiB	912.74 MiB	boot
New Partition #1	ext4	3.91 GiB	---	---	
▽ New Partition #2	extended	2.19 GiB	---	---	
New Partition #3	linux-swap	512.00 MiB	---	---	
unallocated	unallocated	1.69 GiB	---	---	

20. Choose the **Partition | New** menu option and a **Create new partition** window is displayed.

21. Click on the **File system** drop-down list and select **fat32**.

 The fat32 file system is freely supported by a wide range of operating systems. If you need to create files larger than 4 GB, then consider choosing an NTFS file system instead. Modern GNU/Linux distributions can read from and write to NTFS file systems by using the ntfs-3g FUSE driver.

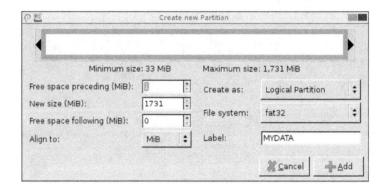

22. Click on the **Label** text entry box and enter a label; for example, MYDATA.

23. Click on **Add** to queue the operation.

24. Choose the **Edit | Apply All Operations** menu option to apply the queued operations to disk.

25. Click on **Apply** to apply operations to disk and click on **Close** to close the apply operations to disk window.

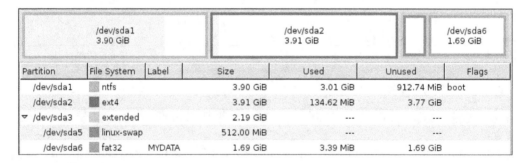

How it works...

This example uses several of the tasks that we covered earlier.

To make room for GNU/Linux we freed up unallocated space by shrinking the operating system primary partition. Then we created a partition with the ext4 file system, and another with linux-swap. The extra step to create a data partition in fat32 format adds flexibility because this partition can be shared with other operating systems.

Since the MSDOS partition table permits up to 4 primary partitions, we could have created the linux-swap and fat32 partitions as primary partitions too. However, this would prevent creating additional partitions in the future. That is why we chose to place these two file systems in logical partitions within an extended partition.

You are now ready to install GNU/Linux. Be sure to choose the manual partition option when installing your distribution. That way you can configure Linux to use the partitions you just created.

The following steps demonstrate how to choose a manual partition layout while installing Ubuntu 12.04.

1. After you have downloaded the distribution .iso file and burned it to a CD, boot your computer using the Ubuntu Live CD.

2. Choose your **Language** and the **Install Ubuntu** option.

3. At the **Preparing to install Ubuntu** screen, click on **Continue**.

4. At the **Installation type** screen, choose **Something else** and click on **Continue**.

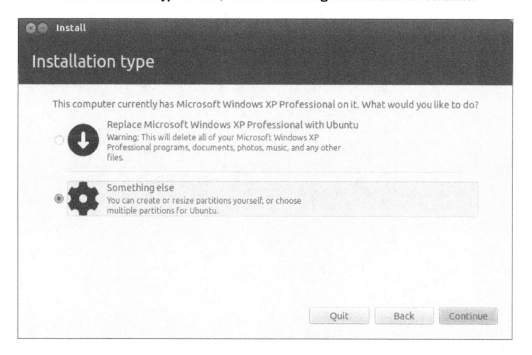

5. Select the **ext4** partition (for example, sda2) and click on **Change....**

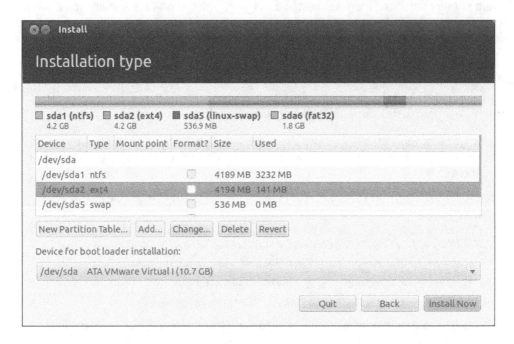

6. Set **Use as** to **Ext4 journaling file system**, **Mount point** to / and click on **OK**.

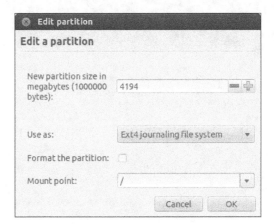

7. Scroll down and select the **fat32** partition (for example, sda6) and click on **Change...**.

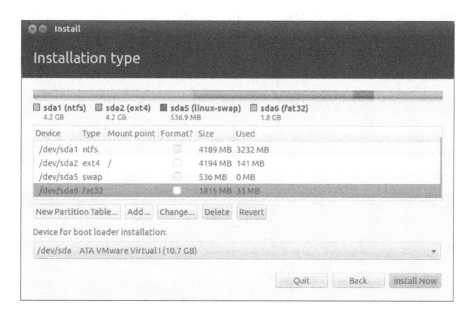

8. Set **Use as** to **FAT32 file system**, type in a **Mount point** (for example, **/data**), and click on **OK**.

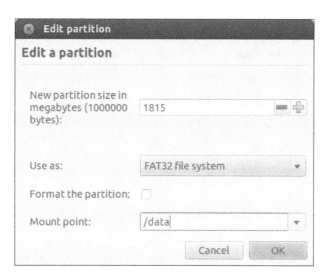

9. Note that you do not need to select the linux-swap partition (for example, sda5) to use as swap space because the Ubuntu installer will do this automatically.

10. Ensure that the **Device for boot loader installation** is correct (for example, **/dev/sda**).

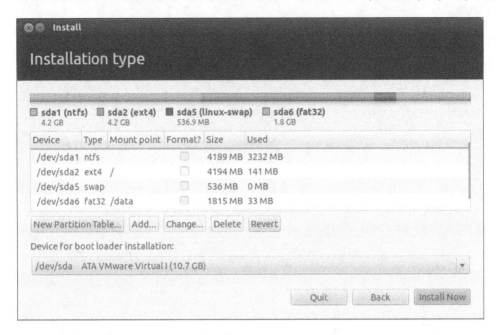

11. Click on **Install Now**.

12. When you are prompted **Do you want to return to the partitioner**, click on **Continue**.

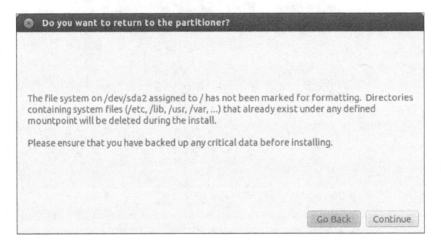

13. Follow the instructions on the remaining screens to choose your location, keyboard layout, your name, computer name, username, password, import accounts (if desired), and when the installation completes click on **Restart Now**.

All data stored in the fat32 partition will be available to both operating systems. In this example Ubuntu installation, the fat32 partition data is accessible in the top level /data directory. In Windows, it is accessible through a drive letter, such as the G: drive.

There's more...

Remember from previous recipes that if you resize a partition containing an NTFS file system, you should reboot into Windows twice. This permits Windows to perform file system consistency checks.

OEM Partition

Some personal computers have an **Original Equipment Manufacturer** (**OEM**) partition. This partition is usually at the start of the disk device and is often involved in the boot process. Most often the OEM partition contains tools to restore your PC to original factory condition. As such we suggest keeping this partition in case you ever need to restore your PC to factory condition.

Adding space to GPT RAID (Become an expert)

Adding disk space to a **Redundant Array of Inexpensive Disks** (**RAID**) can increase the storage capacity of the RAID. With large RAIDs, the **GUID Partition Table** (**GPT**) is often used because msdos partition tables are limited to 2 TB. Since the GPT stores a backup copy of the partition table at the end of the disk device, the GPT must be updated to take advantage of the increased storage capacity. The steps to update the GPT are covered in this recipe.

Getting ready

Add the extra disk space to your RAID. As RAID configurations vary widely in the hardware and software used, we leave the task of increasing the storage capacity of the RAID to you.

How to do it...

1. The following screen shot shows RAID prior to adding the extra disk space:

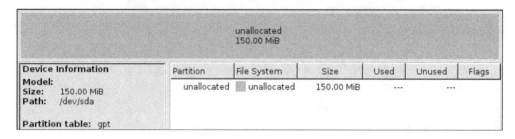

2. Boot GParted with the extra space already added to the RAID.

3. Optionally, if the following window is displayed then click on **Fix**.

 This window is displayed only when the RAID contains no partitions. If you choose **Cancel** or **Ignore** then you will not be able to use the recently added extra disk space.

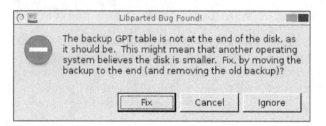

4. Click on **Fix** when the following window is displayed.

 If you choose **Ignore** then you will not be able to use the recently added extra disk space.

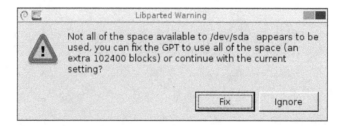

5. The GPT now permits access to all of the RAID capacity.

Partition	File System	Size	Used	Unused	Flags
		unallocated 200.00 MiB			
unallocated	unallocated	200.00 MiB	---	---	

How it works...

When extra disk space is added to RAID, the extra space is not immediately available for partitioning. This is because a GUID Partition Table has a backup copy of itself stored at the end of the device. To remedy this situation, update the GPT so that the backup partition table is moved to the end of the RAID. Then the GPT is able to see all of the extra storage capacity.

There's more...

If you do not fix the GPT, GParted will still show the additional disk space but you will be unsuccessful when applying operations that create or adjust partitions to use the additional disk space.

With today's larger disks devices and with support built into modern operating systems, GPT is taking over from the msdos partition table. One of the main reasons is that an msdos partition table cannot access partitions larger than 2 TB, or partitions that start beyond the first 2 TB of the disk device. Another reason is that GPT supports 128 primary partitions, whereas msdos is limited to 4 primary partitions.

Note that RAIDs that use msdos partition tables do not require this repair step because there is only one copy of the msdos partition table, which is located at the start of the disk device.

Reference information

For more information on RAIDand the GUID partition table, see http://en.wikipedia. org/wiki/RAID, http://en.wikipedia.org/wiki/GUID_Partition_Table.

Rescuing data from a lost partition (Become an expert)

If you delete or otherwise lose a partition and realize that you need some data from the partition, there is still some hope. This recipe describes the steps to attempt data rescue from a lost or deleted partition.

Getting ready

While we hope it never happens to you, if you lose a partition by accidental deletion or by some other method and you do not have a backup of your data, this recipe may help you to rescue data from your partition. To improve the chances of rescuing data, do not write to the partition table by creating new partitions or resizing existing partitions.

This data rescue method supports searching for the following file systems: ext2, fat16, fat32, ntfs, reiserfs, and jfs. If you lost a different file system, then see the *Restoring a deleted partition* section at the end of this recipe.

For this example, we started with a small 100 MB disk device with two partitions containing NTFS file systems. To demonstrate rescuing data, we deleted the second partition (approximately 15 MiB NTFS). The following image shows the partition layout in GParted prior to partition deletion:

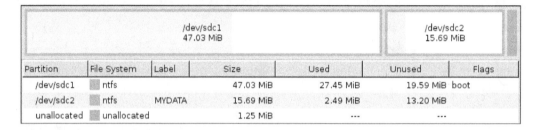

Partition	File System	Label	Size	Used	Unused	Flags
/dev/sdc1	ntfs		47.03 MiB	27.45 MiB	19.59 MiB	boot
/dev/sdc2	ntfs	MYDATA	15.69 MiB	2.49 MiB	13.20 MiB	
unallocated	unallocated		1.25 MiB	---	---	

How to do it...

1. Choose the **GParted | Devices** menu option and select the device with the lost partition.

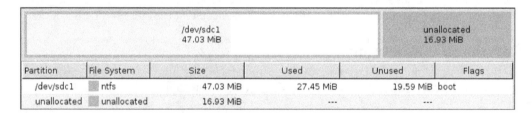

Partition	File System	Size	Used	Unused	Flags
/dev/sdc1	ntfs	47.03 MiB	27.45 MiB	19.59 MiB	boot
unallocated	unallocated	16.93 MiB	---	---	

2. Choose the **Device | Attempt Data Rescue** menu option.

3. Click on **OK** to initiate the disk device scan. Please note that the full disk scan might take a very long time to perform for large disk devices.

4. After the scan has completed, locate the lost partition file system entry in the list of file systems found (for example, the 15 MiB NTFS entry). Click on **View** beside this entry and GParted will attempt to mount the file system in read-only mode.

If your lost partition is not found, then unfortunately you will not be able to rescue the data using GParted. For a different recovery option see the *Restoring a deleted partition* section at the end of this recipe.

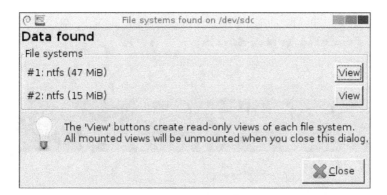

5. With the GParted Live image, a warning window is displayed.

If the warning window indicates **Unable to open the default file manager**, then proceed to the step 6.

If a different warning window is displayed, then there was a problem mounting the file system and you will not be able to view or copy the files in this partition using GParted.

To rescue data from other lost partitions, go back to step 4 and repeat the steps with a different file system entry.

6. In the **Unable to open the default file manager** warning window, make note of the directory where the file system is mounted. The mount point will be in the form: `/tmp/gparted-roview-XXXXXX`

7. Open a terminal window by double-clicking on the desktop **Terminal** icon.

8. Optionally, confirm the contents of the file system using the **ls** command. For example:

    ls /tmp/gparted-roview-6fyXvx

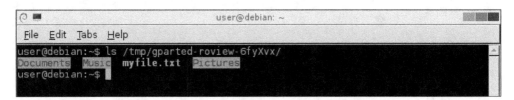

 Note that you can learn more about a GNU/Linux command by using the **man** command. For example: `man ls`

9. Attach an extra storage device, such as a USB flash drive, to the computer and wait several seconds. This permits time for the device to be recognized by the operating system.

10. Enter the `dmesg` command into the terminal window to determine the device name (for example, sdX). For example,

    dmesg

```
 ⟲ ■                              user@debian: ~                              ■ ■ ■
 File  Edit  Tabs  Help
=3
[ 3126.071301] usb 1-2.1: Product: Memory
[ 3126.071303] usb 1-2.1: Manufacturer: Patriot
[ 3126.071305] usb 1-2.1: SerialNumber: 741C4071
[ 3126.158800] usbcore: registered new interface driver uas
[ 3126.159787] Initializing USB Mass Storage driver...
[ 3126.159873] scsi3 : usb-storage 1-2.1:1.0
[ 3126.159928] usbcore: registered new interface driver usb-storage
[ 3126.159929] USB Mass Storage support registered.
[ 3127.162181] scsi 3:0:0:0: Direct-Access     Patriot  Memory          8.07 PQ
: 0 ANSI: 2
[ 3127.168396] sd 3:0:0:0: [sdd] 15663104 512-byte logical blocks: (8.01 GB/7.46
GiB)
[ 3127.169484] sd 3:0:0:0: [sdd] Write Protect is off
[ 3127.169488] sd 3:0:0:0: [sdd] Mode Sense: 03 00 00 00
[ 3127.170414] sd 3:0:0:0: [sdd] No Caching mode page present
[ 3127.170417] sd 3:0:0:0: [sdd] Assuming drive cache: write through
[ 3127.177919] sd 3:0:0:0: [sdd] No Caching mode page present
[ 3127.177924] sd 3:0:0:0: [sdd] Assuming drive cache: write through
[ 3127.187473]  sdd: sdd1
[ 3127.198261] sd 3:0:0:0: [sdd] No Caching mode page present
[ 3127.198266] sd 3:0:0:0: [sdd] Assuming drive cache: write through
[ 3127.198269] sd 3:0:0:0: [sdd] Attached SCSI removable disk
user@debian:~$ ▮
```

11. Make note of the device name of this recently attached storage device (for example, sdd). We will use this device name in subsequent steps.

12. Make a directory to mount the recently attached storage device, by entering the following command in the terminal window.

    ```
    sudo mkdir /mnt/myusb
    ```

13. Mount the USB drive on this directory by entering one of the following commands in the terminal window:

    To mount USB drives as read/write with NTFS file systems use:

    ```
    mount -t ntfs-3g /dev/sdd1 /mnt/myusb
    ```

 The -t option will use the ntfs-3g fuse driver, which permits reading and writing to ntfs file systems. By default ntfs is mounted read-only. Most other file systems are mounted with read/write access by default.

    To mount USB drives as read/write with other file systems use:

    ```
    mount /dev/sdd1 /mnt/myusb
    ```

14. Use the `cp` command to copy files from the lost partition to the USB flash drive. For example, to copy all files, use:

    ```
    sudo cp -v -a -r /tmp/gparted-roview-6fyXvx/ /mnt/myusb
    ```

> Alternatively, if you wish to open a graphical file manager for copying files, position the mouse pointer on the desktop (not over a window), right click to open the **Fluxbox** menu, and then select **File Manager**.

15. Unmount the storage device by entering the following command in the terminal window:

    ```
    sudo umount /mnt/myusb
    ```

16. Wait until the umount command completes, then disconnect the storage device.

17. Click on **OK** to close the **Unable to open the default file manager** warning window.

18. In the terminal window choose the **File | Quit** menu option to close the terminal window.

    If you need to rescue data from other lost partitions then go back to step 4 and repeat the steps with a different file system entry.

19. Click on **Close** to close the **Data found** window.
    This will unmount all of the lost partitions that were mounted when you previously clicked the **View** button.

How it works...

To find file systems on disk devices, GParted uses another application called **gpart** (not to be confused with GParted) to scan the entire disk device for recognizable file systems.

If file systems are found by this utility, GParted displays a window with an entry for each partition file system found. By clicking the **View** button beside the entry, GParted will try to mount the partition in read-only mode. If the mount is successful, you can manually navigate to the mounted file system. Moreover, you can manually mount additional storage in order to store a copy of the data from the lost partition.

When you close the window with the list of found file systems, these temporarily mounted partitions are unmounted.

There's more...

The gpart application used to scan the disk device is not infallible. In some instances, gpart will fail to recognize common file systems. If this happens, you will not be able to use GParted to rescue your data.

Unfortunately the gpart application has not been actively maintained, leaving it behind current advancements in partition tables and file systems. As such, gpart suffers from the following limitations:

- Can find, at most, 4 partitions.

- Does not recognize newer file systems, such as BTRFS.

With these limitations in mind, if you have lost a partition with valuable data, it might still be worth the effort to attempt to rescue the data using the steps in this recipe.

Restoring a deleted partition

If you wish to restore the deleted partition back into the partition table, we suggest you investigate a more powerful command line application called **testdisk**. The testdisk application is included with GParted Live. To learn more about testdisk, see `http://www.cgsecurity.org/wiki/TestDisk`.

Appendix: Tips and tricks

Following are some tips and tricks to help you manage partitions on different devices with GParted.

Maintaining Mac OS X hybrid partition table

Mac OS X uses a hybrid partition table scheme that is a combination of GPT and MS-DOS partition tables. This hybrid partition table scheme is non-standard. When you edit the hybrid partition table, GParted will make the GPT align with GPT standards by writing a single protective entry in the MS-DOS portion of the hybrid partition table. This causes the partition entries in the MS-DOS portion to be lost, and prevents some operating systems from booting, such as 32-bit versions of Windows.

Fortunately these MS-DOS partition entries can be recreated from the GPT partition entries. When you finish editing Mac OS X partitions, open a terminal window and enter the following command:

```
sudo gptsync /path-to-disk-device
```

where */path-to-disk-device* is the disk device you just edited (for example, /dev/sdc).

The gptsync command will copy the GPT partition entries that are below the 2 TB MS-DOS limit into the MS-DOS portion of the hybrid partition table scheme.

Editing iPod partitions

If you wish to repurpose your iPod for use as a RockBox music player, or as a portable GNU/Linux drive, you may wish to edit your iPod partition table. Before editing iPod partitions, you should be aware of the following unusual partition configuration.

Some iPods have a proprietary firmware partition at the start of the device. This partition ID is set to type 0 (zero). A type 0 partition ID usually indicates the partition is empty. In this situation, GParted treats the partition as empty and might use the partition table entry, or overwrite the partition while you are editing iPod partitions. This can overwrite the proprietary firmware, causing your iPod to cease to function as the manufacturer intended.

To prevent overwriting this type 0 partition we recommend that you use the following high-level steps:

1. In a terminal window use the fdisk command line tool to set the partition type to non-zero value (for example, 83).

2. Next, start GParted and perform your partition editing.

3. When finished with partition editing, exit GParted.
4. Finally, use `fdisk` to set the partition type back to zero (for example, 0). Some versions of `fdisk` will warn about setting the type back to zero, but in this case a zero partition id is needed.

Following is a example listing of an iPod partition table with a type 0 partition:

```
user@debian:~$ sudo fdisk -l /dev/sde
Note: sector size is 2048 (not 512)

Disk /dev/sde: 8120 MB, 8120172544 bytes
250 heads, 62 sectors/track, 255 cylinders
Units = cylinders of 15500 * 2048 = 31744000 bytes


    Device Boot      Start         End      Blocks   Id  System
/dev/sde1                1           3       92876    0  Empty
/dev/sde2                4         255     7812000    b  W95 FAT32
user@debian:~$
```

Assuming the iPod is recognized as device /dev/sde, the steps to use fdisk to change the partition id type are as follows:

```
user@debian:~$ sudo fdisk /dev/sde

Command (m for help): t
Partition number (1-4): 1
Hex code (type L to list codes): 83
Changed system type of partition 1 to 83 (Linux)

Command (m for help): w
The partition table has been altered!

Calling ioctl() to re-read partition table.
Syncing disks.
user@debian:~$
```

Use similar steps, as shown above, to set the type back to 0 (zero), instead of 83.

[🔆 If you edit your iPod partitions, your iPod might cease to function as the manufacturer originally intended.]

Adding space to virtual machines

Oftentimes, **virtual machine (VM)** software provides the ability to add more space to virtual disk drives. However, adding more space does not increase the size of the virtual disk drive partitions. This is where GParted can help. The high-level steps are as follows:

1. Configure the virtual machine BIOS to first boot from removable media, such as a CD or USB flash drive.

   For more information on how to configure BIOS, see `http://gparted.org/display-doc.php?name=gparted-live-manual`.

2. Attach GParted Live to the VM as removable media. In some cases you can connect the VM CD drive directly to the `.iso` image file. You might also need to create a new CD device for the VM.

3. Boot the virtual machine.

4. Use GParted to add new partitions or grow existing partitions to use the added space.

5. Shut down the virtual machine.

6. Disconnect GParted Live from the VM.

Using these steps, you can avoid creating a new VM with larger virtual disk drives. This will save time and effort needed to reinstall the operating system and applications, restore the data, and configure the system.

Getting help with GParted

There are several resources available to help you with GParted:

 ▸ Answers to frequently asked questions can be found on the FAQ at `http://gparted.org/faq.php`

 ▸ Assistance with problems is available in the forum at `http://gparted.org/forum.php`

 ▸ New bugs can be reported, and links to existing bugs can be viewed on the bugs page at `http://gparted.org/bugs.php`

For additional information on GParted, see `http://gparted.org`.

Other uses for GParted

The practical applications of GParted are numerous since GParted can be used on a wide variety of disk devices. Searching the Internet reveals many ways people have used GParted to accomplish their goals.

Some of the other uses of GParted include:

- Expanding the memory in Android smart phones
- Migrating operating systems to larger drives
- Preparing disk devices for use with digital video recorders and game consoles

The list of uses for GParted continues to grow.

With these many uses in mind, we hope that this book has empowered you with the knowledge and tools to manage partitions with GParted.

Thank you for buying
Manage Partitions with GParted How-to

About Packt Publishing

Packt, pronounced 'packed', published its first book "*Mastering phpMyAdmin for Effective MySQL Management*" in April 2004 and subsequently continued to specialize in publishing highly focused books on specific technologies and solutions.

Our books and publications share the experiences of your fellow IT professionals in adapting and customizing today's systems, applications, and frameworks. Our solution based books give you the knowledge and power to customize the software and technologies you're using to get the job done. Packt books are more specific and less general than the IT books you have seen in the past. Our unique business model allows us to bring you more focused information, giving you more of what you need to know, and less of what you don't.

Packt is a modern, yet unique publishing company, which focuses on producing quality, cutting-edge books for communities of developers, administrators, and newbies alike. For more information, please visit our website: www.packtpub.com.

About Packt Open Source

In 2010, Packt launched two new brands, Packt Open Source and Packt Enterprise, in order to continue its focus on specialization. This book is part of the Packt Open Source brand, home to books published on software built around Open Source licences, and offering information to anybody from advanced developers to budding web designers. The Open Source brand also runs Packt's Open Source Royalty Scheme, by which Packt gives a royalty to each Open Source project about whose software a book is sold.

Writing for Packt

We welcome all inquiries from people who are interested in authoring. Book proposals should be sent to author@packtpub.com. If your book idea is still at an early stage and you would like to discuss it first before writing a formal book proposal, contact us; one of our commissioning editors will get in touch with you.

We're not just looking for published authors; if you have strong technical skills but no writing experience, our experienced editors can help you develop a writing career, or simply get some additional reward for your expertise.

Network Backup with Bacula How-To

ISBN: 978-1-84951-984-7   Paperback: 60 pages

Create an autonomous backup solution for your computer network using practical, hands-on recipes

1.   Set up Bacula infrastructure.

2.   Back up data and directories

3.   Work with multiple-storage systems

Metasploit Penetration Testing Cookbook

ISBN: 978-1-84951-742-3   Paperback: 268 pages

Over 70 recipes to master the most widely used penetration testing framework

1.   More than 80 recipes/practicaltasks that will escalate the reader's knowledge from beginner to an advanced level

2.   Special focus on the latest operating systems, exploits, and penetration testing techniques

3.   Detailed analysis of third party tools based on the Metasploit framework to enhance the penetration testing experience

Please check **www.PacktPub.com** for information on our titles

Oracle Enterprise Manager Cloud Control
12c: Managing Data Center Chaos

Get to grips with the latest innovative techniques for
managing Data Center chaos including performance
tuning, security compliance, patching and more

Porus Homi Havewala (OCM)   [PACKT] enterprise⊞
PUBLISHING

Oracle Enterprise Manager Cloud Control 12c: Managing Data Center Chaos

ISBN: 978-1-84968-478-1   Paperback: 350 pages

Get to grips with the latest innovative techniques for
managing Data Center chaos including performance
tuning, security compliance, patching and more

1. Learn about the tremendous capabilities of the
   latest powerhouse version of Oracle Enterprise
   Manager 12c Cloud Control

2. Take a deep dive into crucial topics including
   Provisioning and Patch Automation, Performance
   Management and Exadata Database Machine
   Management

3. Take advantage of the author's experience as an
   Oracle Certified Master in this real world guide
   including enterprise examples and case studies

GeoServer

Share and edit geospatial data using open source
server-side software with this book and ebook

Beginner's Guide

Stefano Iacovella
Brian Youngblood   [   ] open source ✳

GeoServer Beginner's Guide

ISBN: 978-1-84951-668-6   Paperback: 350 pages

Share and edit geospatial data using open source serve-
side software with this book and ebook

1. Learn free and open source geospatial mapping
   without prior GIS experience

2. Share real-time maps quickly

3. Learn step-by-step with ample amounts of
   illustrations and usable code/list

Please check **www.PacktPub.com** for information on our titles

www.ingramcontent.com/pod-product-compliance
Lightning Source LLC
LaVergne TN
LVHW080103070326
832902LV00014B/2394